ELIMINATE KITCHEN CLUTTER WITH THE GUIDE THAT GIVES CONCISE PRODUCT INFORMATION *AND* PRACTICAL ADVICE.

My neighbor just spent a small fortune on a convection oven. Are they really worth the money?

Some are. Some aren't. When it comes to spending the big bucks, the Guru will show you how to do it with confidence.

I'd like to buy a new set of knives. But how do I keep them sharp? Are there some knives that stay sharper longer?

The Guru not only rates the best kitchen tools for their quality and value, but also offers helpful advice on how to use and maintain them.

I'd love to have every gadget for my kitchen. But I only have so much space. Which ones will really help me the most?

Starting with the basics, the Gadget Guru leads you from everyday tools that will make your life easier to those products that work great if you've got the space and money.

I'm afraid to spend a lot on new kitchen appliances because new and better ones keep coming out.

The Guru looks at upcoming innovations and designs, and at new products that will soon be available for your kitchen.

The Gadget Guru's Guide to the Kitchen

ALSO BY ANDY PARGH

*The Gadget Guru's Make-It-Easy
Guide to Home Repair*

*The Gadget Guru's Guide
to the Kitchen*

The GADGET Guru's GUIDE TO THE KITCHEN

ANDY PARGH
WITH JOHN KELLEY

WARNER BOOKS

A Time Warner Company

The information provided in this book is based upon sources that the authors believe to be reliable. All such information regarding individual products and companies is current as of July 1998.

Warner Books, Inc., 1271 Avenue of the Americas, New York, NY 10020
Visit our Web site at http://warnerbooks.com

 A Time Warner Company

Printed in the United States of America
First Printing: December 1998
10 9 8 7 6 5 4 3 2 1

Library of Congress Cataloging-in-Publication Data

Pargh, Andy.
   The gadget guru's guide to the kitchen / Andy Pargh, with John
Kelley
     p. cm.
   ISBN 0-446-67431-1
   1. Kitchen utensils—Evaluation. I. Kelley, John. II. Title.
TX656.P37 1998
683'.82—dc21   98-24373
                              CIP

Book design and text composition by L&G McRee
Cover design by Tony Russo
Cover photo by Slick Lawson

Acknowledgments

I have been told over and over again that I have the greatest job in the world. Needless to say, I don't disagree.

You would think that getting to see and play with the latest and greatest new products months before they are unveiled to the general public is the best part of being the Gadget Guru. Well, you would be wrong, as the part of my career I cherish the most is the friendships I have made along the way. There are so many wonderful people that I depend on to make things happen that it is impossible to mention each and every one of them in the manner in which they deserve. But it is their support that keeps everything going like clockwork. There are a few, though, that I would like to take the time to introduce you to and to thank for their ongoing support. My list starts with two Johns: John Lentz and John Kelley.

John Lentz is my advisor, attorney, business manager, and, most important, friend. Because of our friendship, our countless hours spent in meetings or on the phone are not considered work. Every day is a new adventure, and I have to thank John for keeping me on the straight and narrow path.

John Kelley, the co-author of this book and numerous other projects, is the guy who keeps my company cranking out television segments, books, and newspaper and magazine features. He spends almost as much time running around the country as I do. It seems like lately he's spending even more time facing PR people than me—bless him for that! But what makes our time on the road worthwhile is the camaraderie we have established over the years.

Sharon Troth has been with me for more years than I care to remember, through good and bad. She's the organized one who keeps our projects on schedule—a chore that, while sometimes being thankless, is always appreciated.

Terri Campbell is my able assistant, the one who keeps me on schedule—not to mention organized. Not an easy task! Just keeping track of my airline and hotel schedule is a full-time job, not to mention all of her coordinating efforts that keep us running like a well-oiled machine. She also keeps track of my social calendar and constantly reminds me where I have to be and when I have to be there. Her attitude is always positive, which makes her a pleasure to be around.

Then there are the others—not only co-workers, but also friends—I depend on each and every day: Rob and Eric, who keep our massive Internet databases up to date; Jessica (and formerly Julia), who keep our America Online site up and running; Jenny, who has the impossible chore of keeping John Kelley on track; Nancy, who makes sure we can find the products we need and gets them to the right place on time; and Brenda, who organizes my home life and takes care of my most prized possessions. These folks know that, through good and bad, they will always come first.

Others who keep our machine well oiled are Kent, Marie, Jackie, Rhonda, Larry, and Tom. They handle the financials, and not one has yet to disappear to a tropical island.

Roland Woerner has become the adopted son of our Gadget Guru family. My original network producer, his advice and guidance over the years have taught me how to disseminate massive amounts of information and have fun while doing so.

At the *Today* show, there's Jeff, Michael, Linda, Beatrice, Bob, Claudine, DeeDee, Day, Nicole, and Mike, who have shown me what a difference *Today* truly makes. They are also the ones who constantly hear my wild ideas and occasionally support them. Also, let me thank Katie, Matt, Al, and Ann on the weekdays and Jack, Jodi, Janice, and Joe on the weekends—who are not only America's First Family, but have been truly gracious over the years. Trust me, when you have a job that requires you to be at work before the sun rises, not to mention having to be awake and alert at outrageous hours, there is some bonding among co-workers that I could never put into words.

Then there's our magazine side, with Tony, Michael, Kevin, and of course David. These folks have made what could have been tiresome projects fun. They also believed in me and have given my group the ultimate level of support.

There are more, but if I listed them all I would be out of space—and who would buy a book that was one long-winded dedication? Not me!

Oops, I almost forgot my family members—Mom and Dad, Bernie and Maria, Linda and Michael—who have not only been supportive of my numerous ventures but have also contributed to this book. Okay guys, the check is in the mail!

Finally, there's Whisper and Einstein, my four-legged children. I'd write something sentimental about them in this space, but neither one can read. They know I love them.

A wise friend once told me, "If you enjoy your work, you get to play for the rest of your life." That's exactly what I'm doing. My only hope is that those I work with are having as much fun as I am.

To you, the reader, I hope you have as much fun perusing these pages as John and I had putting them together.

Introduction

Of all the rooms in the home, the kitchen is the place where true creativity begins. But that's not what this book is all about.

On your next trip to the bookstore, take a walk down the cookbook aisles and you will see firsthand the abundance of these primers that are available on the market today. For most of them you need to have a fairly high level of kitchen expertise. With this book, there is no experience necessary. That's because, although this book is sprinkled with a few user-friendly recipes, this is not a cookbook per se. It's a manual, a guide to the products that promise to make preparing your favorite recipes easier than ever before.

I remember back in my younger years that it was virtually impossible to walk through a grocery store without being solicited by someone wanting to demonstrate a superlative food product that was prepared with the latest new kitchen device. Why were they successful in selling their wares to passersby? Because the pitch-person could take the time to demonstrate the attributes of a specific item and show you that a dish was so easy to prepare using their product that you would want to use it for each meal. Sounds a bit like snake oil, doesn't it?

If you did purchase the item, it most likely began collecting dust the minute you brought it home.

Today those demonstrations have all but vacated the aisles of the supermarket and are now appearing on the airwaves in the form of infomercials. Are the products found on infomercials and in all of those catalogs we receive in the mail full of hype, or do they truly do the job? How about the ones that are displayed on retailers' shelves and are prominent in their advertisements? The answer is some yes and some no. It is my job to wade through the hype to let you know which products are worth your hard-earned dollar.

That's what this book is all about: knowing which kitchen products work and which ones can truly save you time in order to make your already hectic life a bit easier. Within these pages you will find hundreds of new products, with plain English explanations that cut through all the hype. You will find numerous tips and time savers that I hope you will find useful for years to come. Also included are several buying guides that allow you to get the most for your money by knowing what you are buying before you reach for your credit card. Don't worry, though: I tried my best to keep the book light-hearted and fun to read.

So kick back, relax, and enjoy.

Contents

CHAPTER **2. Pandemonium: Cookware 101 29**

CHAPTER 3. Gimme da Cord: Countertop Appliances **61**

CHAPTER **5. Big-Ticket Items: Ranges, Cooktops, Refrigerators, and Dishwashers 143**

CHAPTER 1

The Right Stuff
Kitchen Essentials

Some say: "What every kitchen needs is a good cook." We say: "Anyone can be a good cook—if they have the right stuff."

For me, the right stuff is having the proper assortment of gadgets to make mincemeat out of even the most complicated kitchen chores.

This chapter is your "stepping-on" point—a road map to the basic "stuff" you need to succeed in the kitchen. It includes everything from spices to dry goods to measuring devices, cutlery, can openers, and colanders, to name just a few. We've also tossed in a heaping helpin' of amazing gadgets designed to make preparing your food easier and fun too.

But that's not all. You will also find a virtual cornucopia of useful tips and information. So whether you're a seasoned chef or just the family's short order cook, sit back, relax, and enjoy. You're in the right place to find the right stuff for all your culinary creations.

Before you get started, remember one point: If you are not a seasoned chef, don't worry. This book is designed to teach you how you can fool your friends and family into believing you really know what you are doing, even if you don't. The right gadget or proper cookware item can transform you into a master chef—even if you have trouble boiling water.

SECTION I

Pantryitis

Our first stop is in the pantry. This is the black hole found in most kitchens that, instead of being a convenience, has become a shrine— a museum of obscure oils, spices, and baking goods collected over the years. While you may use some of the stuff (when you can find it), your mother's allspice from 1965, that mufaleta mix you experimented with in college, and the jar of molasses from your high school trip to Amish country are now more suited for the Smithsonian than for your next meal.

The good news is that you're not alone. Many suffer from pantryitis, and with a little determination and organization it can be cured. The bad news is that you're going to have to let go of the relics and start anew.

So without any further ado, let's clear the cobwebs, grab a trash bag, clean out the cupboard, and get started.

CANNED AND DRY GOODS (CHECKLIST)

- ❏ **All-purpose flour:** A mainstay in any kitchen. Store in airtight canister.
- ❏ **Baking soda:** Jack of all trades. An open box freshens your fridge for six months, puts out grease fires, and can keep your teeth white too.
- ❏ **Baking powder:** Thickens the mix. Store airtight.
- ❏ **Granulated sugar:** No artificial stuff when cooking, please.
- ❏ **Brown sugar:** How come you taste so good? It's great in homemade BBQ sauce.
- ❏ **Cornmeal:** Corn bread, muffins, and casseroles will thank you.
- ❏ **Tomato paste:** For spaghetti and other sauces and stews. Comes in cans or a toothpaste tube–like container.
- ❏ **Plum tomatoes:** When fresh is not an option.
- ❏ **Crushed tomatoes:** Always something to put them in.
- ❏ **Mac 'n' cheese:** Admit it, you love this stuff. Great for a quick meal.

VINO, VINEGARS, OILS, AND MORE (CHECKLIST)

❏ **Wine:** Cooking wines, both white and red, taste awful. Cook with table wines, but use affordable ones under $10. Save the good stuff for the meal.

❏ **Olive oils:** Three types: pure (good), virgin (better), extra virgin (best). Plan on using olive oils (whatever grade) frequently—a whole lot in sauces, stews, grilling, and salads.

❏ **Apple cider vinegar:** Splash some on your chops or other meats. You'll love it. Great on salads too.

❏ **Balsamic vinegar:** Expensive, but worth it. Great on fresh fruit.

❏ **Vanilla extract:** A baker's best friend.

❏ **Honey:** Where would we bee without you?

❏ **Maple syrup:** Vermont's best-tasting export. (Sorry, Ben and Jerry)

❏ **Cooking sherry:** You may not use it, but it looks cool in your pantry.

❏ **Worcestershire sauce:** The mighty marinade. What doesn't it taste good on?

❏ **Soy sauce:** Another tasty marinade. Try low-sodium versions.

❏ **Tabasco:** Yee ha!

SPICES AND HERBS

Mention the word "spice" these days and you're likely to conjure up five singing Brits in oversized tennis shoes. But hey, the Spice Girls have nothing on the pure pleasure you can get from adding a little flavoring to your meal. We've made a checklist of basic spices and herbs for the kitchen. Of course there's a lot more you can add to your kitchen collection, but what are we here, Julia Child? This will be enough to get you started.

Thirteen Essential Spices (Checklist)

❏ Sesame seed
❏ Black pepper
❏ Cinnamon
❏ Cayenne pepper

❏ Crushed red pepper
❏ Coriander
❏ Parsley flakes
❏ Dill weed
❏ Oregano
❏ Nutmeg
❏ Allspice
❏ Seasoning salt
❏ Garlic salt

Ten Herbs (Checklist)

❏ Basil
❏ Cilantro
❏ Dill
❏ Marjoram
❏ Oregano
❏ Parsley
❏ Sage
❏ Thyme
❏ Bay leaves
❏ Rosemary

Most of us store spices either in the cupboard or in a spice rack. Two new products make storing, locating, and dispensing spices easier than ever before. Read on.

Select-a-Spice Carousel from KitchenArt
$40

This lazy–Susan–like device holds 12 different spices in individual containers. Each container snaps in and out of the carousel for easy spice dispensing through its unique quarter-teaspoon dial or flip-top shaker. Even better, the unit can be mounted under a kitchen cabinet, or up to three carousels can be stacked together. It includes common spices and labels (including blanks). This truly wonderful item keeps your spices in one place, and makes them easy to access and dispense.

Seasonart Electronic Spice Rack from Bond/Helman
$50

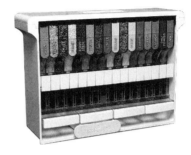

You didn't think the Gadget Guru was going to write a book without electronic devices in it, did you?

The Seasonart is an electronic 10×13-inch spice rack that mounts flat against a wall and holds up to 16 spices. To operate, just slide the measuring chamber to your preferred spice, select a measurement (from ⅛ teaspoon to 1 tablespoon), and push a button. A vibrating motor dispenses the exact amount into a removable shaker. You can even combine multiple spices in the chamber for a perfect blend. Powered by four D batteries or optional AC adapter. Definitely a conversation piece.

➤**Tip:** Scatter a bay leaf or two in your kitchen cabinets to keep critters out.

SECTION II
Tools of the Trade

Now that your pantry is prepped, it's time to stock up on the tools you need to tackle any job. Let's begin with one of the most important items for any cook: knives.

Professional cutlery, once the province of great chefs and circus acts, is now readily available to the consumer. Of course you pay a price for quality, but knives, like cookware, are an excellent investment. Spend a bit more money on the front end and you'll get years of performance over the long haul.

The good news is that unless you're Wolfgang Puck or Emeril Lagasse, four knives (chef's, slicer, utility, paring) are all you truly need to survive in the kitchen. And while you're at it, you may consider purchasing a set of good-quality steak knives, as they can end the embarrassment of your guests having to saw their food.

MORSEL OF KNOWLEDGE

In the early seventeenth century, French statesman and resident royal Miss Manners Armand Jean du Plessis, aka Cardinal Richelieu, supposedly ordered all sharp points to be shaved off his dinner knives. Why? It was to end the unsightly habit his male dinner guests had of picking their teeth with his pointy knives after a meal. Quite naturally, this inspired hostesses throughout France, thus paving the way for blunt knives to become a part of the table setting.

ESSENTIAL KNIVES

- **Chef's:** This is the big daddy, and the one you will use the most. It measures either 6, 8, or 14 inches and is used for chopping and slicing.

- **Slicer:** Features a long blade with a pointy tip for carving the turkey, roast, or fish dishes.

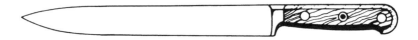

- **Utility:** Smaller knife for chopping tomatoes, peppers, etc.

- **Paring:** Usually a 3-inch blade. Used for delicate cutting like apple peeling and removing stems from veggies and other fruits.

OTHER KNIVES OF NOTE

- **Boning:** Also called a fillet knife, features a thin 6-inch blade with a sharp tip for filleting fish or trimming meat.
- **Bread:** Usually 8 to 10 inches long. Bread knives are best with a serrated type of blade. Instead of having a smooth blade surface, a serrated blade looks like teeth. It allows you to smoothly cut thin or thick slices of just about any type of bread or loaf. Consider this a necessity if you own, or are planning the purchase of, an automatic bread machine.
- **Poultry shears:** Like a pair of scissors but in a reduced size. Very sharp and able to cut through the joints of your bird.
- **Kitchen scissors:** To prevent ruining your expensive knives, keep a pair of kitchen scissors nearby. Great for cutting through those "microwavable" bags.
- **Cleaver:** No, not June, Ward, Wally, and The Beaver, but a superstrong large blade that is a staple at butcher shops, Asian kitchens, and Three Stooges movies! Cleavers make it easier to cut square chunks of meat and other items for stir-fry and stews.

➤**Tip:** When you chop herbs like parsley, use both hands to rock the blade of the chef's knife back and forth like a seesaw over the herbs, without lifting the blade from the cutting board. This gives you a more uniform cut and better control of the knife.

KNIFE-BUYING GUIDE

- **Construction:** Carbon steel or high carbon stainless steel knives are the most durable and easiest to keep sharp.
- **Tang:** No, not the preferred drink of astronauts, but a term for how far the knife blade extends into the handle. The best knives have a full tang, which means the blade extends the length and width of the handle. Make sure the tang is held together by at least three rivets for maximum hold and durability. Brass or nickel rivets indicate good quality, as they don't rust or loosen.
- **Forged:** Dating back to the days of the Japanese samurai, forged knives are made the old-fashioned way: by hand. They are also the most expensive.
- **Moistureproof handles:** Need I say more?
- **Comfort:** The most obvious factor is the most important. Feel the knife in your hand; make sure it's balanced and handles well.

Best Bargain Knife Set with a Twist: Ekco's 8-piece Cutlery Set with Built-In Cutting Board Model No. 1166012

$23

"Hey Guru, I'm on a budget and don't really care about tang, forged steel, and all that other stuff. What do you suggest?"

This set from Ekco includes six knives (chef's, slicer, boning, utility, parer, and tomato) with serrated edges that never need sharpening and plastic polymolded handles so you can put them in the dishwasher. It has a wooden storage block and a unique detachable 9¾×6¾×½-inch wood block cutting board that hides away when not in use.

**Best Value Professional
Knife Set: Chicago Cutlery
7-Piece Block Set
Model No. BL4701**

$270

This 7-piece carbon steel construction knife set includes a 3-inch parer, 4½-inch steak/utility, 5½-inch utility, 8-inch slicer, 8-inch chef's knife, 10-inch steel sharpener pole, and a wooden storage block, all in one nice tidy package.
Even better, each knife is guaranteed forever by Chicago Cutlery.

**Ultimate Cutlery Set:
LamsonSharp Gold Forged
10-Piece Block Set
Model No. 39770**

$625

This is definitely one of our favorite companies. This 10-piece forged carbon steel knife set includes a 3-inch paring knife, 5- and 6-inch utility knives, a 6-inch boning knife, an 8-inch bread knife, a 6- and an 8-inch chef's knife, a 10-inch slicer, and a sharpening steel-and-wood block. Each blade features a full tang and three brass rivets for strength and is also backed by a lifetime guarantee. And, to top it off, they are made right here in the USA!

KNIFE CARE TIPS

- Never put your expensive knives in the dishwasher. Excessive heat and moisture damage the handles, and dishwashing chemicals destroy the blade's finish.
- Always wipe the knife clean after use.
- Beware of acidic food, as it can slowly ruin your knife. If you need to cut a lemon, use a cheap knife for this purpose or clean the knife immediately afterward.
- Sharpening wheels on low-cost can openers and other devices may not work and can warp your blades. If you use an automatic sharpener, use a high-quality model.
- As knives begin to wear, use a sharpening stone or rod to keep them in good shape.
- And remember: Dull knives can cause accidents in the kitchen.

Unique Bread Knife: OXO Natural Grip Bread Knife

$12

Looking more like a hacksaw than a bread knife, this ergonomically designed cutter makes slicing through your favorite loaf easier than ever. It's great for crusty breads like French bread, and its L-shaped handle fits the natural position of your hand and wrist. Other features include a serrated stainless steel edge that never needs sharpening.

Bagel Cutlery: The Bagel Biter

$30

There's nothing more irritating or dangerous than trying to cut a bagel in half. One slip, and it's off to the emergency room. To the rescue comes the Bagel Biter—a guillotinelike device equipped with

a supersharp LamsonSharp blade that makes the perfect slice every time. To use, just place the bagel in the base, get your fingers out of harm's way, and push down—it's really that easy. The unit is stylishly constructed out of maple and has an extrawide base for stability.

A Knife Sharpener that Works: Chef'sChoice Diamond Hone Model No. 110

$55

Although most electric knife sharpeners, especially those found on low-cost can openers, have awful sharpening stones that do more damage than good to your cutlery, there is one diamond in the rough—the Chef'sChoice Diamond Hone sharpener. This model features an electronic sharpening wheel that you can feel safe using with higher-quality knives. It has 3 slots that allow you to quickly and easily accomplish a three-stage sharpening process that goes from coarse to medium to ultrafine, giving you the sharpest blades around. It uses industry-preferred diamond stone abrasive sharpening wheels to create a strong arch-shaped edge on your cutlery. When I first saw this product, its representative, in an effort to show me how well his product performed, asked me to bring in my dullest knife from home. He placed it in his machine for a few seconds. Then, to my surprise, in order to show how his product gave even my lousy knife a razor-sharp edge, he raised his pant leg and began shaving hair off his leg. The funny part was that this was not the first time he had given this demonstration, as evidenced by the hairless patches scattered on his leg. Although I definitely do not recommend trying this at home, his demonstration caught my attention, and proved his point—literally!

THE CUTTING BOARD DILEMMA:
WOOD, PLASTIC, GLASS, OR ANTIBACTERIAL?

It's the great kitchen debate. Where do you cut your food? On one side, pundits say a wood block is the only surface to use, and on the other scientific prophets insist that a coating of antibacterial chemicals prevents contamination. Who's right?

The answer is that it really doesn't matter as long as you pay attention to what you are doing. The bottom line: Make sure you wash your cutting board (whatever the surface) after every use—especially after you cut poultry. Then be sure to place it in the dishwasher. Uncleaned wood surfaces can transfer bacteria, but so can antibacterial cutting boards. So don't be lured into a false sense of security by the protective coating. Buy what you want, but remember to wash after each use.

➤**Tip:** You'll shed no more tears when you slice an onion if you place the tasty bulb in ice water for a few minutes before cutting.

Best Cutting Board for Politicians: Bemis Reversible Cutting Board

$27

Wood on one side and plastic on the other, this cutting board is perfect for those who can't decide which surface to cut on. It's great for the fence-straddling politician too. Featuring a resin core permanently bonded to a ½-inch-thick block of maple wood, it measures 9⅛×15 inches and is dishwasher safe.

GROCERY SHOPPING TIPS

1. **Shop around:** Love cheese? Look carefully in three places in your store for the same product—all with different prices. The dairy case will usually have staple cheeses such as cheddar, Swiss, and Monterey Jack, prepackaged at the lowest price. The deli and cheese tables may have exactly the same products, but you'll pay more. Know what you want, and shop all three areas for the best price.

2. **Pay attention to package sizes:** Does "10% More Free" get you to buy extra product? Some products, beverages in particular, are already in larger packages, giving us more than the label says, to insure that they don't run the risk of being underweight, which is sure to get the FDA's attention and fines. Don't think that little extra isn't built into the price already! So when you see the "extra free" label, make sure it's not the same-sized package with a special label.

3. **Don't be fooled:** "New" or "New and Improved" labels can mean the product has just come out or has been made better—or it can mean a new color, new flavor, or just a tweak in the formula. There is no word more coveted than "new" for a product on the supermarket shelf. The government knows this, so it limits use of the word on labels and packaging to six months. You probably won't be able to tell if the "New and Improved" label is true, unless you can find an old one to compare it with. Check the ingredients and the nutritional data.

4. **Check the calories:** Are you buying those expensive no-fat products but gaining weight? Have you switched to frozen dinners with hardly any fat and eat only no-fat cookies, but your weight hasn't changed? You are not alone. Remember that fat, besides delivering terrific texture for a product, is also a bulking agent. When fat is taken out, it must be replaced with another bulking agent. A lot of the time, it's sugar! Check out the ingredients and calorie counts; you might be surprised. You might be better off eating smaller portions of the "regular" version.

5. **Don't trust "tastes great!" claims:** "Tastes great" or "improved flavor" claims always make me ask, "According to whom?" You should ask the same question before you switch brands and buy. This is one of those marketing slogans that drives me nuts! If it tasted so bad before, why should I believe you now? The average package in the supermarket has about $\frac{1}{17}$ second to attract our attention, so the manufacturer will try anything to make us stop, look, pick up the product, and put it in our cart.

6. **Read the nutritional label (not the brand):** Healthy Choice started it, and everyone else followed. Now there are dozens of brands containing the word "healthy." Under new label regulations, manufacturers can't incorporate the word "healthy" into their brand names, but the brands that were on the shelves before the regulations were enacted are grandfathered and can continue to use the word. Some brands are more healthful than others. Always read both the nutritional label and the ingredients list, and judge for yourself how healthful the product is.

7. **Think twice about rebates:** Fewer than 6 percent of shoppers ever redeem rebates or mail-in offers. But they're a great incentive to buy a product we usually don't or to purchase multiple packages to comply with the offer. Before you put the products in your cart, decide whether or not you really will redeem the offer.

8. **Enter contests without buying the product:** Products that offer you a chance of winning a free trip to Hawaii are especially appealing in midwinter. And even though the package says in very small type that you don't have to buy the product to enter, you feel your chances have to be better if you do. Wrong! Strict state regulations on contests prohibit companies from showing a preference toward purchasers. If the contest appeals to you, but the product doesn't, don't buy it. But do enter the contest. Your chances are just as good, and you haven't bought a product you'll never use.

9. **Don't believe the scanner:** Do you relax when you see a sign at the checkout that says, "We guarantee our scanner price is correct or you get the product free?" Well, don't. While systems are getting a lot better, many errors still occur at the checkout. Don't blame the cashier or the scanner. The problem is with the prices being put into the computer system. For specials, especially on the first day of a sale, bring the newspaper ad with you and watch the register's display to make sure the scanned prices are correct.

10. **Don't shop when you're hungry:** Don't go shopping when you're hungry or cranky or in a bad mood! Our supermarkets are getting better and fresher all the time, so when we walk in, we are bombarded with great colors, tastes, and smells. Eat first, shop later.

Compiled by Phil Lempert, the Supermarket Guru, and a distant relative of the Gadget Guru (just kidding). He is an expert on shopping and all things food. You can visit his Website at www.starnews.webpoint.com/food/shguru.htm or read his columns or catch him on the *Today* show.

SECTION III

Stir, Peel, Whip, Beat, and Measure

A Pacifist's Guide to Kitchen Utensils

If you stop and think about it, the kitchen is a wonderful place to relieve stress. Where else can you legally beat, whip, and mash things and then produce something so beautiful and tasty? But what really makes the kitchen so special is all the unique "weapons"—I mean devices—you need to prepare a meal. This section will help arm you with all the right utensils to attack and defeat any recipe you're brave enough to take on.

ESSENTIAL KITCHEN UTENSILS (CHECKLIST)

- ❏ **Wooden spoons:** Chefs prefer wooden spoons to metal to stir and taste-test with. Wooden spoons don't conduct heat, and they don't transfer a metallic taste to your special sauces.
- ❏ **Whisk:** Stop scrambling eggs with a fork! A whisk makes them lighter, fluffier, and sooo much better tasting.
- ❏ **Ladle:** Do you tip your pots to serve soups or sauce? Get a ladle; it's much easier and causes less of a mess.
- ❏ **Skimmer:** Or a slotted spoon. Looks like a ladle but allows you to scoop and leave the liquids and fat behind.
- ❏ **Spatula:** Metal or plastic or both. Remember the movie *Stripes*?
- ❏ **Cheese grater:** Everything tastes better with cheese.
- ❏ **Combination grater/slicer:** From cheese to easy hash browns, this is a wonderful tool as long as you know where the food stops and your knuckle starts.
- ❏ **Potato masher, potato ricer:** Throw away those powdered mashed-potato mixes and make your own. (See box below.)
- ❏ **Pasta server:** From the pot to your plate, the easiest way to serve pasta.
- ❏ **Vegetable peeler:** Probably the ultimate kitchen gadget.
- ❏ **Apple corer:** An amazing device.
- ❏ **Ice-cream scoop:** Stop bending all your spoons.

❏ **Measuring cups and spoons:** Kitchen essentials.

❏ **Can opener:** Definitely a necessity; screwdrivers only worked in college.

❏ **Garlic press:** Yes, some really do work.

❏ **Meat thermometer:** Unless you have X-ray eyes or are clairvoyant.

❏ **Colander:** Definitely wash everything before you eat it—you don't know where it's been.

HOW TO MAKE PERFECT MASHED POTATOES

One of the best parts of my job is that I get to meet interesting people from all over the country. One of them is my good friend and frequent *Weekend Today* show contributor Donata Maggipinto. Although her day job is as the Food and Entertaining Director for the Williams Sonoma catalog, she regularly appears on the show to demonstrate great new recipes that even we can duplicate at home. Although some of her stuff is a little off the wall, such as her basil-filled ice cubes for strawberry lemonade, I promised her that if she let us use her mashed-potato tips, I would give her catalog a plug. Here goes: Williams Sonoma—an excellent resource for the hottest gadgets, appliances, and cookware in the housewares industry! Call them at (800) 541-2233 for a free copy. See, I keep my word! Now, here are the tips:

- Any type of potato can be used for mashed potatoes. White, yellow, or red will make creamier mashed potatoes; baking potatoes produce fluffier mashed potatoes.
- The easiest way to make velvety smooth potatoes is to use a potato ricer—and the potatoes needn't be peeled. Place cooked, quartered, peeled, or unpeeled potatoes in the ricer, squeeze the handles together, and watch as perfect mashed potatoes come out—without the peels.
- Please note that a potato masher will produce lumpy, fluffy mashed potatoes—which gives them a true potato taste. (Note: Unless you use a masher after you use the ricer, your potatoes will look like spaghetti.)
- Never use a food processor to mash potatoes—you'll end up with a gooey mess.

- Make sure to dry potatoes well after cooking by draining them thoroughly, then returning them to the pan for a minute or two, turning them so they don't scorch. This will ensure creamy (not watery), fluffy mashed potatoes.
- Mashed potatoes will hold up to an hour before serving. Place them in the top pan of a double boiler or in a heatproof bowl placed over (but not touching) simmering water.
- Try stirring flavored oil, chopped herbs, horseradish, shredded cheese, garlic, or pesto into mashed potatoes for a delicious twist on the traditional.
- Leftover mashed potatoes make delightful potato pancakes. Form into patties and grill on a stovetop griddle. Serve with pesto or sour cream or alongside roast chicken.

KITCHEN UTENSIL SHOPPING GUIDE

Best Way to Stop Reading This Book: Metro Marketing's First Kitchen, a 77-piece Kitchen in a Box

$150

Like Cliffs Notes for our own book, the folks at Metro Marketing have assembled the First Kitchen Collection, a 77-piece bargain-basement collection of everything you need to prepare and cook a meal—all in one box.

Now, we're not telling you to put this book down, or to ignore the other products listed within these pages, but if you're in a hurry and need everything right now, you may want to check this assortment out. Even if you do get it, there's still a lot of good stuff in this book. (Check out chapter 3 to find out about countertop appliances.)

With too many items to mention, this all-in-one collection includes pots, pans, knives, graters, roast racks—even a teakettle, not to mention every gadget listed on pages 15 and 16. Of course you get what you pay for, but if you're a college student or new homeowner on a budget, who are we not to report on a neat idea? It also makes a great housewarming gift.

Potato Masher, Peeler, Ice-Cream Scoop, and Corer: OXO Good Grips

$5–$10

OXO's kitchen utensils shine because of their ergonomically designed slotted/padded grips, which make any chore in the kitchen easier than ever. Each item features a hole for hanging and looks great too.

No-Brainer Meat Thermometer: Artex Steak and Poultry Buttons

$4

Forget confusing meat thermometers that take an MIT degree to decipher. Two products, the Steak and Poultry Buttons from Artex, tell you what you need to know. To use, just plug one of the specially calibrated stainless steel reusable thermometers into your meat. The Poultry Button has a dial and is labeled with one word: DONE. Need I say more? The Steak Button has a dial with settings for Rare, Medium, and Well. Any questions?

Marvelous Meat Thermometer: Norcross Pro Chef Fork

$25

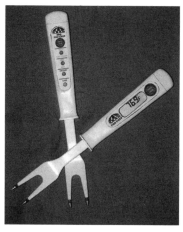

Now here's a novel idea, a meat fork combined with an electronic thermometer. This 6-inch-long fork features electronic probes and an LCD display on the handle that reads food temperatures in 2 to 6 seconds. Great for outdoor, indoor, or even microwave cooking. To use, just insert its tines into the food for a few seconds and read the temperature. It doesn't get any easier than this!

Salt and Pepper Shaker: Chef'n Pepper Ball and Salt Ball

$20/ea

Definitely a gadget-lover's delight! This stylish acrylic see-through ball features two protruding levers that look like shoehorns, which, when squeezed, grind the pepper or sea salt and dispense the results directly onto your food. The Pepper Ball has an adjustable grind for fine or coarse ground pepper. Each ball holds 5 ounces and has a sliding door for easy refilling. The balls come prefilled with peppercorns or sea salt. If nothing else, they are great conversation pieces.

Garlic Peeler: The Elan E-Z Rol
$8

Sometimes the simplest products are the best, and when it comes to peeling garlic there's no better tool than the E-Z Rol. To use, just place a clove of garlic inside its rubber tube and roll it on a hard surface. The pressure and the garlic oil relieve the garlic of all its skin, leaving a shiny clove ready for mincing. It works, it's easy, and your hands don't smell for days afterward! You really have to see it to believe it.

Measuring Spoons: KitchenArt Adjust-a-Measure
$10

When we walk the aisles of the housewares and gourmet trade shows, we see huge booths displaying hundreds of innovative items made by numerous companies. Well, honestly, we have to wade through these hundreds of items just to find the one or two that it makes sense to put on the air or in the newspaper. That's what separates KitchenArt from the pack. Instead of a huge booth packed with products, it conserves cash by renting only a small, out-of-the-way booth and displaying only the best of the best. This is a small company and does not manufacture a vast array of kitchen gadgets—only a few, high-quality, well-thought-out items. That's why we like these people—when they introduce a new product, it's usually worth taking a look at. That is definitely the case with the Adjust-a-Measure assortment.

Just three of these innovative measuring spoons replace more than 14 of the traditional measuring spoons and cups. The spoons can hold either liquid or dry ingredients. Each spoon has five measurement increments and features a sliding top that locks into place at each measurement. Models include an Adjustable Teaspoon with 5 increments from ⅛ to 1 teaspoon, an Adjustable Tablespoon with 5 increments from 1 teaspoon to 1 tablespoon, and an Adjustable Cup, which measures from ⅛ to ½ cup. These three items can help relieve the clutter in your kitchen drawers.

KitchenArt Easy Measure

$10

Another unique product from KitchenArt is the Easy Measure, a clear spice jar–like container that features a measurement setting for a pinch—one of the great mystery measurements in kitchen lore. Just fill the container with your favorite spice, dial its top to Pinch, press, and voilà! Your dish is blessed with this mystery measurement. The dispenser also delivers 1/8 and 1/4 teaspoon measurements.

Fat Skimmer: Fats Off Soup Scoop

$13

This hard plastic ladlelike device not only is ideal for transferring soup from the pot to the plate, it separates the calories and the fat from the substance by featuring a grid on its cupped bottom. It works based on the principle that fats and oils rise to the top. To use, just press the scoop straight down into the soup until the fat has been trapped and goes into the ladle collector. Once the ladle is full, empty and repeat several times in different areas of the soup until virtually all the bad stuff is gone. You can then use the collector to serve the soup. Even better, the grid can be removed for skimming thick stews and sauces.

Bodacious Baster: Artex Fat Separating Baster/Skimmer

$3

Looking more like something out of your doctor's office than a kitchen gadget, this rubber-gripped test tube device is designed to separate fat from juices for healthy basting. To use, just place the tip in the juices from your roast, turkey, and so on, squeeze the handle, and its plastic Lexan tube sucks the juice and fat in. Once inside, the fat juices separate (in about 3 seconds), leaving the low-fat meat juices in the bottom and the bad fat in the top so you can easily rebaste with the good stuff and discard the fat. Great for skimming soups and stews too.

Killer Colander: Yaffa Hands Free Colander

$5

When this nifty device first hit our office, just about everyone commented on its practical uses.

This plastic colander features a hook that wraps around your kitchen faucet so you can drain pasta or wash your vegetables without sinking the colander in dirty water or clogging it by setting it in the sink basin.

Best Manual Can Opener: The Safety Can

$20

Yes, you've seen it on those late-night infomercials, and some lucky person probably made zillions of dollars on it. This manual can opener does something no others can do—it eliminates sharp edges from opened cans and keeps the top from falling into the can itself.

Unlike other can openers, which cut the inside rim, the Safety Can penetrates the outer seal of the can's lid, making a clean cut just below the top. The lid then lifts off easily every time, sans sharp edges. And you'll never have to fish for the lid again. Definitely a must for families with youngsters.

Best Electric Can Opener: The Krups OpenMaster

$35

This product was originally introduced under the Moulinex name. Well, now Krups owns it, and like the Safety Can, it allows you to open a can by penetrating its outer seal. But instead of manually cranking its handle to open a can, all you need with this electrically powered marvel is a press of a button. When my dogs (Whisper and Einstein) hear it in operation, they run to the kitchen thinking that it's Canned Food Night! It is truly one of the better products of the decade.

SECTION IV

A Harbinger of More Great Gadgets

If necessity is the mother of invention, then the kitchen is the neediest place on the planet. After all, where else could you find products like the Mouli, the Veg-a-matic, and the Ginzu knife? Meet some of our favorites on the following pages.

MORSEL OF KNOWLEDGE

The housewares industry holds a special place in my heart, as it is the only industry that officially recognizes the gadget as a category of products. The first Gadget Guru was a Frenchman fittingly named Gaget. He was part of the firm that built the Statue of Liberty. This industrious fellow came up with the idea of selling miniature Liberty Statue souvenirs to Americans in Paris. Americans soon brought them back and began calling them "gadgets" around 1860. At the same time the industrial revolution was fostering growth in small electric devices for the kitchen that became known as—YOU GUESSED IT—gadgets. You can find other tasty morsels like this one in Charles Panati's *Extraordinary Origins of Everyday Things* (Harper & Row, 1987).

Pickle Perfection: Progressive's Pickle Jar

$15

Here's the problem with pickle jars: You unscrew the top, and if you are lucky, you don't spill the smelly pickle juice all over the place. Then you reach in and pull out a pickle, and BOOM, more pickle juice all over the place. Yes, you can use a fork, but for some odd reason we usually don't.

That's where this product comes to the rescue. This is a unique, two-chamber acrylic canister that, when tilted on its side, allows the juice to drain into a holding area so you can remove the contents without getting your hands wet. It's also ideal for storing olives and cherries. Now you know, beyond a shadow of a doubt, that for every problem, there is a solution.

Parmesan Cheese Grater: OXO Rotary Cheese Grater

$10

Pouring canned Parmesan cheese on your pasta dishes is a crime! Just don't do it. Add a little quality to your life, and buy a Parmesan cheese grater. One of the simplest is the OXO Rotary Cheese Grater. Just load a small chunk of fresh Parmesan (available at the dairy department of your favorite supermarket) and grind away directly into the recipe or onto the finished product, and watch even the worst sauce suddenly sing out with joy. The OXO grates easier than any other table grater we've tested. It also can be used to store the unused portion in the fridge, and it comes apart for easy cleaning.

Car Wash for Your Lettuce: The Emsa Salad Washer and Dryer

$29

Although salad-spinning bowls are the easiest tool for washing and preparing tossed salads, most of them have one problem—they spin the bowl in only one direction. This means that it takes a long time and a substantial amount of elbow grease to rid the lettuce of unwanted water.

The Emsa Salad Washer and Dryer puts a new spin on salads by replacing the standard turning crank with a winding rip cord. This cord allows the bowl to spin first in one direction, and when the cord catches, it automatically reverses to the opposite direction—meaning that the water is propelled away from the salad. It has a 5-quart capacity.

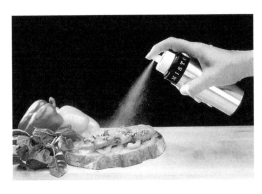

Olive Oil Storage: The Misto Olive Oil Sprayer

$20

Fill this stainless steel–looking canister with olive oil or other favorite cooking liquids or marinades, pump the cap to pressurize, and spray away. It atomizes the oil into a fine mist. Great for grilling or just prepping your pans for cooking, the Misto holds up to 3½ ounces. Hey, it can also be used with liquid hair sprays—but not on your food.

Food Life Preserver: The Food Buddy

$20

Looking like an air freshener, this nontoxic 4½×5-inch device goes in your refrigerator and keeps your food fresher and crisper longer.

How? you ask. Inside the Food Buddy is an all-natural mineral substance called silica that, when activated (when you put it in a microwave for 30 seconds or in the sun for 3 hours) absorbs moisture, thus preserving your fruits and vegetables for up to a week

or more than normal. The Food Buddy lasts up to four years and helps keep odors at bay too.

Ultimate Gourmet Kitchen Scale: The Soehnle Evolution

$145

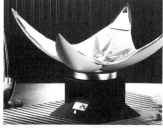

Okay, so I won't even attempt to properly pronounce this manufacturer's name. It really doesn't matter, because they make great stuff. To prove this point, just check out this user-friendly kitchen scale. Even if you don't measure anything in your kitchen, this decorative scale will add class to your operation. When not in use, it looks like a tulip. But simply fold down its sides, and it blooms into a scale with an electronic LCD monitor and 24-inch square measuring area.

Juice Extractor: Frieling Citrus Trumpet

$5

It doesn't play "Dixie," but simply twist this 3½-inch metal "trumpet" into a lemon, orange, or other citrus fruit, and squeeze the juice, sans seeds and pulp, on or into your favorite foods.

Oven Mitt: Tuckers' BurnGuard Mitt
$30

Not all oven mitts are created equal, as evidenced by Tuckers' new BurnGuard mitt. The BurnGuard's extralong mitt covers from fingertip to elbow and is designed to withstand temperatures up to a sizzling 900 degrees F. The BurnGuard mitt, truly a technological marvel, accomplishes these feats because it is made of DuPont Nomex and Kevlar as well as a layer of VaporGuard, which protects the user from hot liquids, grease, and steam—even when the mitt is wet.

The mitt is machine washable and is promised to last 15 to 20 times longer than standard mitts. Tuckers' BurnGuard mitt is currently available and retails for $30. You may consider buying two and keeping one beside the fire extinguisher.

Storage Solutions: SnapWare Dry Food Storage
$5 to $11

Dry food represents over 56 percent of weekly grocery purchases, and because most storage containers are not airtight, Americans throw away an estimated 25 percent of their food due to spoilage. To the rescue comes SnapWare—a new line of storage containers that are 100 percent airtight. Each container features gasket-lined snap tops and a clear plastic design guaranteed to preserve your foods. SnapWare comes in a variety of sizes and shapes to hold anything from cereal to coffee to spices. And because the containers are affordably priced, you can buy them in a variety of shapes and sizes.

CHAPTER 2

Pandemonium

Cookware 101

From cooking on a stick to nonstick cooking, cookware has evolved into one of the most important, if not necessary, categories in the kitchen. It's also the most confusing—especially when it comes to selecting exactly which set of pots and pans is right for you. Walk into any department or gourmet store, and it's literally PANdemonium, with more shapes and sizes of pots and pans than you would have ever imagined. With pans that are anodized, Calphalon, Circulon, chromium, copper, and nickel-plated, you would think you're at a science fair instead of a cooking store.

In fact, there are seven different categories of cookware—each with its own set of pros and cons. Making matters even more confusing, within each of those seven categories there are at least two subcategories, which means that if you actually tried to figure all this out you'd be as crazy as we are here at the Gadget Guru world headquarters. Definitely not a good thing!

But let's face it, as consumers, we want the best bang for the buck for our cookware dollar. All we want is something that works without our having to take the time to learn how it works. Like the old adage says: "You don't have to know how to build a car to drive it." Of course, how well it works and how long it lasts depends on what you buy and how you treat it. You may not have to change the oil or rotate the tires on a sauté pan, but its life could depend on how you *season* it—doing what the manufacturer recommends the first time you use it. Because there is such a vast array of these items, choosing them is best compared to selecting an automobile. After all, you can own a Yugo or a Mercedes, and you can own a basic aluminum pan or a hard-anodized, stainless-lined nonstick pan. They will both do the job—but the latter will most likely heat more evenly, be easier to clean, and last years longer.

Many of us have never purchased cookware ourselves. Most of our pots and pans are comprised of hand-me-downs and gifts. Sure, you registered for selected pieces for your wedding, Mom donated lovely 1950s pieces to your collection, and you purchased a nifty fryer at your neighbor's garage sale, but in general, shopping for cookware is not exactly on our agenda as something to do on a sunny Saturday afternoon.

This chapter will arm you with all the firsthand knowledge you need to get the cookware best suited for your lifestyle. We'll cover every category, with special emphasis on nonstick coatings—the greatest advancement in cookware since the handle! We'll also take a look at the sticky world of nonstick warranties and find out why even some manufacturers agree that there is no such thing as a lifetime warranty.

The following section takes us inside the oven with a look at bakeware—everything from roasters to cookie sheets to cake pans. We'll also share some simple recipes, and, of course, we'll end with a journey through all the great gadgets, specialty cooking devices, and exotic gizmos that can help you cook and bake your way to the top. So sit back, relax, and get ready to start cooking!

SECTION I

Cookware Primer

The most important thing to remember when you select cookware is that it CAN seriously affect your meal. Why? Because cooking is a science, and science dictates that certain metals heat better than others. And since certain metals heat better or more evenly than others, your meals will cook better in pans designed with conduction-friendly metals. Got that?

Simply stated, the rule of thumb is: The better the pan, the better your meal.

Let's first take a look at the different types of pots and pans, and then we'll investigate specific categories to help you find the perfect match.

THE FABULOUS FOUR: COOKWARE BASICS

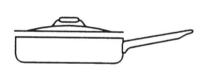

Skillet: This has sloping sides that allow you to slide food off the pan easily. You will need two: one smaller, 7- to 8-inch-diameter pan for omelets and smaller fare; and one deeper 10- to 12-inch-diameter pan for veggies and other creations.

Frying or sauté pan: This is the one Moe, Larry, and Curly know best. This pan is deeper, with larger sides to keep grease from splattering. When you shop, it's a good idea to select one with a companion lid—you'll need it for specific recipes. You may consider a heavy-duty cast-iron fryer (see "Other Cookware of Note") (but keep it away from Moe, as he'll just use it on Larry and Curly).

Stock pot: Get at least an 8-quart soup/stockpot for making your soon-to-be-famous chili and soup concoctions. You'll also find it handy for boiling pastas. Look for pots that come with steamer basket and/or pasta basket inserts.

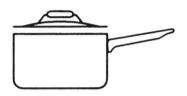

Saucepan: It is recommended that you have two saucepans with lids: a 2-quart (for heating all those Campbell's Soups and Minute rice mixes you keep on hand) and a 3-quart for spaghetti sauce, rice, and more.

Other Cookware of Note

Dutch oven: Usually has a 5-quart capacity, is oval-shaped, and includes a lid. A Dutch oven is ideal for stews, braised meats, and other slow-cooking items. It can be used in the oven or on the stovetop.

Double boiler: This is a two-piece pot that, although you may not use it every day, has its uses. The lower level holds water, which is heated and steams the upper pot, which nests on top. My favorite uses for a double boiler include melting chocolate or caramel, whisking egg yolks, and keeping mashed potatoes warm without burning.

Cast-iron skillet: A staple in the South, a cast-iron skillet gets better with age, as it actually seasons itself over time. However, it is imperative that before its first use you season it by heating a little oil in it for a few minutes (see manufacturer's instructions). A well-seasoned cast-iron skillet is a true nonstick cooking utensil. Because cast-iron skillets can take more heat, they are ideal for searing steaks and blackening your favorite fish as well as for baking the best corn bread on the planet. Drive south and get yourself one.

Butter warmer: I highly recommend investing in one of these. This tiny saucepan typically has a spout-type area on its side for pouring out its contents. It's great for melting butter or heating BBQ marinade.

So, now that you can identify the shapes, let's look at the pros and cons of each type of composition.

CATEGORIES OF COOKWARE AT A GLANCE

Aluminum

Pros: The most common and least expensive of all cookware. Aluminum pans typically conduct heat quickly and evenly and provide a good product for the price. Available both plain and with nonstick coating. Most aluminum pans are lightweight and easy to handle and can be purchased with colored exteriors. When you shop, opt for nonstick.

Cons: Because they are inexpensive, some varieties of aluminum pans (those typically found on the bargain tables at discount stores or in supermarkets) can be of poor quality. Stains can be difficult, if not impossible, to get out. Not considered an investment for the long haul.

Buying tip: The thicker the pan the better. Cheap lightweight pans are just that—cheap. When you shop, read the label and remember: The lower the gauge, the thicker the pan (see "Cookware Q&A" on pages 36–38 for more information on gauge ratings). A nonstick low-gauge aluminum pan is functional for everyday use. When it comes to aluminum cookware, the old adage "You get what you pay for" holds true.

Stainless Steel

Pros: Very durable, and because of its mirror finish aesthetically pleasing. New nonstick coating technology called Arc-Spraying and the addition of aluminum or copper discs on the stainless steel pan's base make this the cookware on the move. Tri-metal or tri-ply pans are an excellent choice. Resistant to chips, cracks, and dents. Will not corrode.

Cons: If there's no nonstick coating it can take a little elbow grease to keep these pots and pans clean; grab the SOS or Brillo pads. A stainless steel pan without any special bottom treatment can be a poor heat conductor. The price goes up when other metals are added to the bottom.

Buying tip: Look for 10 gauge or lower (for thickness), an 18/10 (see "Cookware Q&A" for more information on ratings) or higher chromium-to-nickel ratio, with an aluminum, copper, or tri-ply disc on its base for even heat distribution.

Hard-Anodized

Pros: Charcoal-gray-colored, very durable cookware; it has a surface twice as hard as stainless steel for better heat conductivity. Nonstick hard-anodized pans have proven to be almost twice as abrasion resistant as plain aluminum nonstick pans. Available with or without nonstick coatings.

Cons: You pay to play. Dishwashing detergent can harm the surface; read specific manufacturer information for care tips. Most recommend hand washing only. Hard-anodized pans can be expensive.

Buying tip: Hard-anodized cookware is the best bet for the serious home cook or anyone who wants durability, even cooking, and easy-to-clean cookware. Make sure the cookware is thick—but if you opt for a thinner piece, make sure it has one of the better nonstick coatings.

Copper

Pros: The cookware of choice for gourmet chefs; both functional and attractive enough to hang on the wall. Copper is the best conductor of heat.

Cons: Expensive and requires frequent maintenance: After prolonged use, copper pans will require re-tining or reshaping.

Buying tip: Don't be fooled by inexpensive copper-plated cookware. A good rule of thumb is: If you can easily afford it, it's not copper!

Glass

Pros: Looks cool; available in multiple tints. Easy to view the contents of what you're cooking.

Cons: Poor heat conductivity. Difficult to store without breaking. Just okay for slow cooking.

Buying tip: If you are on a budget, give glass a look. If not, keep the glass in the oven. Makes better bakeware than stovetop cookware.

Cast Iron

Pros: For blackening or searing, nothing beats cast iron. Durable material that retains heat well. Cooks food evenly.

Cons: Bulky, heavy, and hard to handle.

Buying tip: A staple more in the South than in the North—must be all that fried chicken!

Enamel on Steel

Pros: Decorative colors over steel are aesthetically pleasing. Okay for slow low-heat cooking.

Cons: Poor heat conductivity. Very thin metal.

Buying tip: Fashion has its place. Is it on the stovetop?

COOKWARE Q & A

Q: Is it better to buy a set of cookware or individual pieces?
A: That depends on your cooking habits. For busy people, a good set of nonstick cookware is a timesaver. Cookware can be purchased in a matched assortment. You can always add specialty items like omelet pans or cast-iron skillets to your collection when they're needed. For the more serious chef, a good rule of thumb is: Experiment with different types of cookware. Copper, for instance, is the gourmet's choice, as it is perfect for cooking in various high temperatures as well as low heat for sauces—but it is expensive. Hard-anodized cookware cooks stocks and soups more thoroughly than copper. Our best advice is: Unless you have an unlimited budget and can afford a fully matched set of the best, then buy piece by piece, as you need it.

Q: How important is the thickness of cookware?
A: Very—in fact, it's a major factor in determining performance. The thickness of the material is referred to as its gauge. As a standard, the gauge measurements range from 3 to 16. Don't let this confuse you; the smaller the number, the thicker the material. Common sense tells us that the thicker the cookware, the more durable it is and the more likely it is to hold its shape over the long run. If you get a piece that has too high a gauge rating, it is more likely to generate hot spots. However, a heavier pan will take longer to preheat and cool down.

Q: How do I determine the quality of stainless steel cookware?
A: The quality of stainless steel is determined by three factors. The first is its nickel and chromium content, which is described by a fraction like 18/0, 18/8, or 18/10. The 18 stands for chromium, which is always the same; the 0, 8, or 10 is the amount of nickel. The greater the nickel content, the better the pan. For instance, an 18/10 stainless steel pan is better than an 18/0 pan. The second quality test is the pan's thickness or gauge. In general, the lower the gauge number, the thicker the pan. A 10-gauge pan is generally accepted as the standard. The most important quality feature on a stainless steel pan is the thickness and quality of the disc on its base. Since stainless steel is a poor heat conductor, a copper or aluminum disc is essential to cook foods properly. Aluminum discs 3 mm and larger are best: for a copper disc, a 1-mm or larger base is best. Which is better? For heat control choose copper, for retained heat aluminum.

Q: What are tri-ply stainless steel pans?
A: Tri-ply pans are a combination of three metals: stainless steel for style, and copper or aluminum or both for conductivity, all in one pan. Our favorite is All-Clad, the inventor of tri-ply.

Q: What is hard-anodized cookware?
A: Recognized by its industrial charcoal look, hard-anodizing is a scientific process that changes the composition of aluminum to make it twice as hard as stainless steel. Underneath the surface is an aluminum core that provides even heat conductivity throughout the pan, including its walls.

Q: Do I really need a nonstick pan?
A: It depends. For a healthier diet, good nonstick pans eliminate the need for much of the butter or oils to cook your food, therefore reducing calorie and fat. For that reason alone, having one nonstick sauté pan or skillet is a good idea. For pots and saucepans, nonstick can greatly reduce the time it takes to clean your cookware as well. However, some nonstick pans can be damaged in high heat situations and cannot be put in the dishwasher—meaning that it is important to read the restrictions before buying. So it really depends on what your needs are. For most of us, time is of the essence; that's why I recommend nonstick. But for some of us, a meal is not a meal until you've made a mess. A well-made heavy-gauge set of pans without nonstick coatings is still an excellent option.

Q: Why don't professional chefs use nonstick pans?
A: The easy answer is that most restaurants and hotels have full-time human dishwashers and giant machines to clean the cookware—which damages nonstick cookware. However, more and more professionals are using the high-end hard-anodized nonstick cookware not only for its food release properties, but because it conducts a wide range of temperature settings extremely well.

Q: What's the best nonstick coating?
A: The best and most expensive coatings are the three-coat systems like Dupont's Autograph series and Whitford's Excalibur. Also notable are T-Fal's Armaral and DuPont's SilverStone Select and Xtra line. But note that a superior coating on a low-gauge or inexpensive pan is useless. The coating and the pan have to be quality matched for food release to work properly.

Q: Do nonstick coatings wear off?
A: Yes. While hard-anodized aluminum pans and Arc-sprayed stainless steel pans maintain their nonstick qualities longer than

plain aluminum nonstick, steel, or glass pans, no pan, regardless of its warranty, can claim to keep its nonstick qualities forever. Remember, though, that the pan is not ruined when its nonstick capabilities end. That's where nonstick sprays such as PAM come to the rescue.

Q: Will kitchen utensils ruin my nonstick cookware?
A: Yes. Utensil abrasion and overheating can affect nonstick durability, especially with plain aluminum nonstick pans, which are soft. Most cookware companies offer plastic "nonstick-friendly" kitchen utensils with softer edges. It's a good idea to purchase a set to use with your nonstick cookware. Again, read the manufacturers' instructions before buying so that you know what you are getting into.

Q: Do nonstick coatings get in my food?
A: Well, maybe—but don't worry about it. Depending on the type of coating, tiny particles can wear away. But, you will probably never notice it, as nonstick coatings are inert, nontoxic, and deemed safe, and must be approved by the FDA before coming to the market.

A WORD ON WARRANTIES

No nonstick pan can keep its nonstick coating over a lifetime. So why do many manufacturers guarantee their pans for a lifetime? There's a tricky and somewhat deceptive line between a pan's nonstick coatings and its ability to release food. Most of these manufacturers claim their pans will always release food, as opposed to NOT lose their nonstick coating. The bottom line, however, is that regardless of the length of warranty, all nonstick pans gradually lose their nonstick capabilities. How much depends on the quality of the pan. A good pan will last you a long time—a cheap pan won't. But in this case, don't let a lifetime warranty decide your purchase.

➤**Tip:** Question: How many pans do you get in a 7-piece set? Answer: usually 4. Why? Because some marketing genius figured out that the lids count as pieces. So even if you buy a 10-piece set, you may only get 4 or 5 pans. Remember, it's a 7-piece set, not a 7-pan set. Is this a great country or what?

SECTION II
Notable Cookware Collections

Best Value Nonstick Cookware for Folks in the Fast Lane: T-Fal's 9-Piece Armaral Sovereign Collection

$100

This aluminum cookware set is coated with four layers of T-Fal's granite-textured Armaral nonstick substance. Each piece features an embedded steel disc to prevent warping, and T-Fal provides some of the most durable and low-cost cookware on the market.

The collection includes a 1-quart and a 2-quart covered saucepan, a 9½-inch frying pan, and a 5-quart Dutch oven and comes in a variety of colors (midnight, fern, pearl).

Best Tri-Ply Nonstick Cookware Set: All-Clad 7-Piece Stainless Nonstick
$400

From the creators of tri-metal pans come these 18/10, double-layered stainless steel pans with a third heat-conductive aluminum core that extends from the base of the pan to its sides.

Add to that a triple coat of Whitford's top-of-the-line Excalibur nonstick coating, and you have one of the most durable nonstick pans in the business.

The set includes an 8-inch frying pan, a 2-quart saucepan with lid, a 3-quart saucepan with lid, and a 6-quart stockpot with lid. Other features include extralong cool touch handles connected by two sturdy stainless steel rivets.

Best Value Nonstick Stainless Steel Cookware: Farberware Millennium 7-Piece Set

$150

This 18/10 professionally designed extrathick stainless steel set features a 1-quart and a 2-quart covered saucepan, a 5-quart covered Dutch oven, and a 10-inch skillet.

Each pan features a DuPont SilverStone three-coat nonstick surface, aluminum and stainless tri-ply base, stainless steel lids, and cool-touch handles.

Best Value Nonstick Hard-Anodized Cookware Set: Circulon Hi-Low 8-Piece Collection

$200

This cookware incorporates unique circular high/low grooves, which are embedded inside the pan's cooking surface, for durability. It also has DuPont's top-of-the-line nonstick Autograph coating.

It includes a 1-quart and a 2-quart covered saucepan, a 5½-quart covered stockpot, a 7-inch French skillet, and a 10-inch French skillet.

Another Hot Nonstick Hard-Anodized Set: Calphalon 8-Piece Cookware Set

$310

Probably one of the most recognized names in cookware, Calphalon invented the hard-anodized category. Although pricey, this collection of nonstick cookware will last a lifetime.

The set includes an 8-inch and a 10-inch omelet pan, a 5-quart saucepan with cover, a 2½-quart and a 4½-quart saucepan, and a suede pan holder that fits each pan.

SECTION III

Bakeware

The oven is the magician's hat of the kitchen. Put something flat and uninteresting in and pull something amazing out—like a rabbit, or a cookie or a loaf of bread. Okay, bad analogy. Anyway, bakeware is a vital part of any kitchen. Baking, broiling, and roasting is a science—one that involves circulating hot air in an enclosed space to cook food.

The heat-conductive materials needed in the oven differ somewhat from those on the cooktop. Most noticeable is the prevalence of glass and ceramic bakeware. Although it is a poor heat conductor on the stovetop, glass (or treated glass like Pyrex and Corning Ware) is an excellent choice for the oven for exactly the reason that it's not good on the cooktop. Radiant heat seeps through glass, so in the oven it helps prepare your meal more thoroughly. On the cook-top, escaping heat hinders preparation.

This section features a checklist of essential baking items and an analysis of the different types of bakeware, and, once again, it leads us on a treasure hunt—this time, for the hottest roasting pans, cookie sheets, and other bakeware for your own kitchen magician's hat.

BAKING AND ROASTING ESSENTIALS

Here's what you need for the oven:

Cookie sheet: A flat pan with ½-inch edges for—you guessed it—baking cookies, biscuits, and the like.

Jelly roll/cookie pans: A flat 10×15-inch cookie sheet with a rim around it for making jelly rolls, toasting nuts, reheating foods, toasting almonds, or baking cookies.

Casserole dishes: Glass or ceramic dishes for casseroles, pies, and other culinary delights. Purchase bowls and rectangular dishes labeled Pyrex or Corning Ware.

Muffin pan: A 12-cup pan for premixed or homemade muffins and cupcakes.

Cake pans: Two round 9×2-inch pans and a 9-inch square cake pan for brownies.

Loaf pans: For bread and meatloaf, a 6-cup pan will do.

Cooking racks and grids: Nifty gadgets for roasting in the oven and for baking cookies.

Pizza pans: Everyone needs a round pizza pan.

Roasting pan: A pan for fowl, meats, even deep-dish lasagnas. Most have a rack or recessed drip tray that keeps fats away from the meats. A smaller oval-shaped pan is adequate for small meals. If you entertain frequently or have a large family, get a larger rectangular roasting pan.

CATEGORIES OF BAKEWARE

Aluminum

Types: Plain, nonstick, anodized.

Pros: Excellent heat conductor, rustproof.

Cons: More expensive, nonstick coatings can be damaged.

Steel

Types: Plain, nonstick, carbon-based enamel on steel, stainless.

Pros: Inexpensive, less flimsy than aluminum.

Cons: Warping due to extreme heat, rusting over time, poor conductor of heat.

Insulated

Types: Plain, nonstick, air-insulated, aluminum.

Pros: Helps prevent burning, more efficient distribution of heat.

Cons: More expensive, does not crisp as well.

Glass

Types: Plain, treated, nonstick, ceramic.

Pros: For serving dishes, glass is ideal because you can cook in them, freeze them, microwave them, and serve in them too. Ceramics or treated glass like Pyrex offer even more durability and better heat transfer.

Cons: Glass breaks. In fact, high heat can shatter inexpensive glass dishes in the oven. If the pan walls are too thin, heat escapes easily.

➤**Tip:** Spend a few extra bucks on sturdy bakeware that won't warp, scratch, or rust.

MORSEL OF KNOWLEDGE: THE SPIT RUNNER

In the fifteenth century, English terriers known as Spit Runners were trained to run in place on a primitive conveyorlike pulley system connected to a spit over the fire. This relieved the chef of the family from having to turn the meat on the spit by hand.

SECTION IV

Bodacious Bakeware: A Buyers' Guide

Bakeware with Feet: Wearever CushionAire Pro

$18 to $25

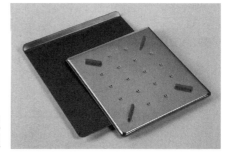

These nonstick coated insulated pans feature two layers of steel

with an air pocket sandwiched in between, which helps prevent burning and facilitates more even baking. But what really separates this bakeware from the pack is its silicon-based cooling feet, which allow you to place a hot cookie sheet or cake pan on your expensive countertops or tabletops without scorching them. Available in a 14×16-inch cookie sheet, 10×15-inch jelly roll pan, a 12×16-inch baking sheet, a 9×13-inch covered cake pan, and a 9-inch round cake pan. Check them out; your countertops will thank you.

A Double-Duty Cookie Pan: Farberware's Reversible Muffin Pan/Cookie Sheet
$20

This cool 11×17-inch cookie sheet pulls double duty. Flip it over and it becomes a muffin pan, complete with 24 indentations for making muffins!

Its nonstick surface ensures that your tasty treats slide off every time, and its air-insulated surface also guarantees against scorching them.

From the Oven to the Tabletop: Pyrex 3-Piece Bake N Serve Casserole Basket Set
$15

Introduced in 1915, the Pyrex brand of treated glass bakeware is still a mainstay in any kitchen.

This unique 3-quart oblong baking dish is perfect for casseroles and desserts and comes with an airtight plastic cover for storing meals. Even better, it also includes a rattan serving basket so you can literally bake and serve in the same dish, while protecting your tabletop.

Jenny's Oatmeal Chocolate Chip Cookies

(Makes 2 dozen)

Jenny Walker is John Kelley's assistant. This book would not be possible without her pestering manufacturers and collecting all the art, graphics, and press material needed for such an undertaking. Besides, Kelley couldn't find his keyboard without her. How she finds the time to make cookies is a mystery.

EQUIPMENT NEEDED: cookie sheet, hand mixer
PREPARATION TIME: 30 minutes

INGREDIENTS
- 1 cup shortening
- 1 cup sugar
- 1 cup brown sugar
- 2 eggs
- 1 tsp. vanilla
- 1½ cups flour
- 1 tsp. salt
- 1 tsp. baking soda
- 3 cups oatmeal
- 1 cup chocolate chips

PREPARATION
- Preheat oven to 375 degrees F.
- Grease a cookie sheet.
- Use a hand mixer to cream shortening and sugars.
- Beat eggs and vanilla in a separate bowl and add to creamed mixture.
- Sift together flour, salt, and soda in another bowl and add to creamed mixture. Mix until blended together.
- Add oatmeal and chocolate chips and stir with a spoon.
- Drop teaspoon-sized spoonfuls on greased cookie sheet.
- Bake for 10–12 minutes or until lightly browned.

Mom's (Madeline Pargh's) Squash Casserole

(Serves 6)

I was one of those children that loved vegetables. I still do! When Mom would take my brother and me to the corner lunch counter, he'd order a burger and fries and I'd order the vegetable plate. He still has not forgiven me for this. At home, while I'd eat my veggies first, he'd painstakingly save his for last. My mom is one of those great cooks who has the knack of grabbing anything in the fridge or pantry and whipping up a veritable feast within minutes. One of my favorite Mom recipes is her soon-to-be-famous Squash Casserole. It's easy to prepare and I'm sure you'll find it a true delight as a side dish for any meal. For a different taste, try substituting eggplant for squash—it is equally as good!

EQUIPMENT NEEDED: food processor, saucepan, sauté pan, and casserole dish
PREPARATION TIME: 45 minutes

INGREDIENTS
- **5 yellow crooked-necked squash**
- **2 onions**
- **2 tablespoons margarine**
- **2 eggs**
- **¼ cup bread crumbs**
- **Salt**
- **Pepper**

PREPARATION
- Preheat oven to 350 degrees F.
- Peel and slice squash and one onion, then cook in a small amount of water in a saucepan for about 10 minutes, or until tender. Drain excess water.
- Dice remaining onion and sauté with margarine in sauté pan until lightly brown.
- Add sautéed onion with cooked squash and other onion to a food processor and chop.
- Add eggs, bread crumbs, salt, and pepper to food processor. Pulse a couple of times.
- Put all ingredients into a greased casserole dish. Sprinkle some bread crumbs on top and bake for 30 minutes.

Timesaving Bakeware: Corning Ware's Classics 6-Piece Bakeware Set

$20

This line of ceramic glass bakeware is great for oven cooking, table-top serving, microwaving, or freezing. It looks good too, with matching patterns of fruit on each dish. The set includes 1-, 2-, 3-, and 5-quart covered casserole dishes with lids, a 4-quart oven roaster, and an extralarge 6-quart covered deep roasting pan. Best of all, Corning Ware is dishwasher safe.

Best Value Roasting Pan and Rack: Metro Marketing's Nonstick Roasting Pan with Rack

$50

Elevating your bird or other meat on a rack over a roasting pan is a great idea, as it allows you to braise potatoes, carrots, and other veggies while you cook your main course. This combination will also make sure that fats drip away from the meat.

This heavy-duty aluminum nonstick roasting pan features a removable V-shaped roasting rack that holds your bird or other meat. The rack holds up to a 20-pound bird, and its roasting pan features a riveted handle for easy lifting.

Howard's Happening Frito Pie

(Serves 5 to 6)

Howard Kelley, John Kelley's brother, is a cultural photographer who travels the globe documenting everyday folks. Whenever possible, he feeds them his Frito Pie—except when he's climbing Mt. Everest; then his food comes from an easy-to-open packet or can.

EQUIPMENT NEEDED: 2-quart casserole dish, skillet
PREPARATION TIME: 30 minutes

INGREDIENTS
- 1 roll of Pillsbury croissant dinner rolls
- 1 pound ground beef, or substitute ground turkey, or vegetables
- 6 ounces taco seasoning (any packaged kind)
- 1 onion (any variety), diced
- 1 green pepper, diced
- 1 garlic clove, minced
- 1 pint sour cream
- 1½ cups grated cheese (cheddar or Monterey Jack with jalapeños)
- salt and pepper to taste
- 1 large bag of Fritos (about 16 ounces)

PREPARATION
- Preheat oven to 350 degrees F.
- Grease a 2-quart casserole dish with butter.
- Line the bottom and sides with croissant dough and pinch the seams together.
- Brown meat in the skillet and add taco seasoning.
- Put beef in casserole dish and layer in half of all other ingredients except the Fritos.
- Add a layer of crushed Fritos; then add remainder of ingredients.
- Top with crushed Fritos and decorate on top with remaining croissants.
- Bake, uncovered, for 20 minutes, and serve with salsa and *cervesa*.

Great Idea Roaster: Artex Roast Rack with Juice Reservoir

$25

This steel roasting rack makes basting easier than ever with its unique angled drip pan, which channels the juices to a holding reservoir mounted on its side. This way you can easily dip a spoon in the reservoir and baste your bird or other meat without the hassle of removing a big roasting pan, tilting it sideways, and fishing for juice.

Double Your Pleasure Baking Rack: The Double Decker Baking Rack

$25

Has this happened to you? You've ordered a few pizzas for a houseful of kids and they arrive cold. You attempt to place them in the oven to reheat, but there's not enough room. Now there's a solution to this dilemma: The Double Decker Baking Rack. Bake four pizzas or dozens of cookies at the same time with this extender rack, which doubles the capacity of your oven. To use, just assemble the three-shelf extender and place it in your oven on top of one rack. That's it. You now have four shelves for cookie sheets, pizzas, and more. Even better, the rack removes and stands alone, so you can cool your creations too. It saves money too, as you have to heat only one oven, not two.

SECTION V

Hot Pots, Specialty Cooking Apparatus, and Everything In Between

Sibyl's Favorite Pan: Progressive's Everything Pan

$80

For all your cooking needs, this unique stainless steel pan has multiple personalities. It's a broiler, fryer, steamer, and sauté pan, all in one. It comes with a lid and a basket attachment for steaming, another for frying; or you can just sauté in it.

The pan is large enough to hold a 12- to 15-pound bird or roast and has a tri-ply bottom that allows you to cook on the stovetop or in the oven. It's also a great gift for someone just starting a kitchen.

World's Most Convenient Spaghetti Pot: VillaWare One-Pot Pasta & Sauce Cooker

$80

This ingenious, 8-quart stainless steel cooking pot with drop-in colander is unlike anything else on the market. One side of the colander is cut out to allow the insertion of an included wedge-shaped, 1-quart cooking pan. The pan slides into the water, allowing you to cook your famous spaghetti sauce while you boil your pasta—all in the same pot. You can cook your entire meal on the same burner.

Other features include a glass cover and a steamer tray that slips into the colander for the steam cooking of vegetables, clams, shrimp, fish, and other delicate items.

Pasta Pot for the First-Timer: Metro Kane's Pasta Time

$70

If you are tired of tossing pasta against the wall to see if it's done, then check out this pasta pot. Because even if you can't boil an egg, you can make perfect pasta with this unique 6-quart pot. It has a built-in timer on its lid with a bell that rings when the pasta is cooked. It features a removable stainless steel colander as well as the correct cooking times for 28

different pastas listed inside its lid. All you have to do is add water and pasta, twist the timer, and wait. It's festively decorated in Italy's red, white, and green colors.

Dad's (Eugene Pargh's) Easy Seashells Pasta Recipe

(Serves 4–6)

When I was growing up, Sunday was Dad's Day—to cook, that is. While lunch was either fresh corned beef sandwiches and potato salad straight from Schwartz's Deli, or hot sandwiches made on the grill, for Sunday dinner there was only one choice: Dad's Seashells. Little did I know then how trend-setting my dad truly was, as he was preparing pasta dishes well before they were fashionable. Every time I make this dish, I have vivid memories of my childhood. When you try this at home, be sure to add a bit of Tabasco for an added kick.

EQUIPMENT NEEDED: cast-iron skillet or other skillet, pasta pot, chef's knife
PREPARATION TIME: 20 minutes

INGREDIENTS
- **24 ounces medium seashell pasta**
- **1 onion**
- **1 green pepper**
- **2 tablespoons olive oil**
- **1 large can (16 ounces) tomato sauce**
- **sugar**

PREPARATION
- Cook seashells in pasta pot.
- Chop onion and peppers.
- Put olive oil in cast-iron skillet and brown onions and pepper.
- Add tomato sauce and a pinch of sugar to skillet. Season to taste and stir.
- Mix in drained pasta shells and cook uncovered in the skillet for 10 minutes.

Every Pan's Friend: Circulon's Pan Companion

$20

One of our favorite trade shows is the International Housewares Show in Chicago. The bad news is that it takes place in January—usually when the thermometer is at its lowest point. But inside the McCormick Place Exhibition Center, you can stay warm eating your way from booth to booth while manufacturers are touting their latest innovations. The only problem with this show is that this exhibition center was recently expanded—and they completely redesigned the show. You may think that this is not a big deal, but John Kelley and I are creatures of habit. We had the show's layout memorized and could plan our days' ventures well in advance. Our favorite area was in the basement, which we called the gold-carpet area. While upstairs in the higher-rent areas you could find the extravagant booths, downstairs in the basement were the smaller, stripped-down booths. These were our favorites. The reason was that the bigger companies with the huge booths had big budgets and hired public relations companies to pitch us products. The lower, less desirable floors were usually reserved for the mom-and-pop companies that typically could not afford the luxury of retaining a PR company. They also often had more innovative items—those you could not find anywhere else. Well, as you could have guessed, with the expansion of this show, this floor has disappeared, and the innovative small companies have been blended into other areas of the show. Yes, they are still there, but we have to walk farther to find them.

Several years ago, we saw the Pan Companion hiding away in the now nonexistent lower level of the Housewares Show. It was so cool that we immediately put it on the *Today* show and wrote about it in our syndicated newspaper column. Now the Pan Companion has hit the big time and is part of cookware giant Meyer Corporation's Circulon line of cookware. The Pan Companion will work with most other lines of cookware as well.

What is it? The Pan Companion is a unique cooking accessory that clips inside the lids of your cookware. The clip allows the lids to hang on the side of the pan while you are cooking. Each set includes 4 wires that fit stockpots (1-quart through 16-quart), and two wires for sauté pans (1-quart through 12-inch). This eliminates your needing to set a lid on a countertop as well as messy condensation. Instead, you just hang the lid on the side of the pan. No muss and no fuss!

Best Cooktop Wok: Joyce Chen Pro Chef Excalibur Series Nonstick Wok

$45

Stir-fry meals are not only healthy, they are easy to make too. The problem is that many woks (both electric and cooktop models) are too thin and flimsy to achieve the high heat necessary to give your stir-fry the flavor found at local Chinese restaurants. To be honest, it's just about impossible to achieve restaurant heat in a wok on a stovetop, but considering all the countertop appliances you have fighting for space, a stovetop wok is usually a better choice than a countertop wok.

Joyce Chen's 14-inch heavy-duty wok sits on any cooktop and has the weight (2 mm) and carbon steel aluminum tri-ply construction needed to achieve higher temperatures for a tasty stir-fry meal. It's also coated with Excalibur nonstick surface for durability and is easy to clean up. So forget carryout, and do it yourself!

A Pressure Cooker with a Sunroof: T-Fal's Safe2 Visio Pressure Cooker

$140

Pressure cookers make mincemeat out of cooking times. Even better, you can just toss in your ingredients and walk away—the pressure cooker does the rest.

Pressure cookers cook food by turning water into steam in an airtight container. The steam's volume pressurizes the container, cooks the food, and releases just enough steam through a valve at the top of the pan to prevent an explosion.

Almost any type of meat or vegetable can be cooked in a pressure cooker. They are especially good for stews.

But forget all that; T-Fal's Visio pressure cooker is just plain cool. It's the world's only pressure cooker with a 4-inch viewing window that lets you watch the whole process. I know what you're thinking: Why would you want to watch steam and pressure? I don't know, maybe it's a guy thing, but it's really neat. If that's not enough, the cooker also features T-Fal's Armaral granite-textured nonstick coating for easy cleanup and has an embedded stainless steel disc to protect it from warping.

Ultimate Pressure Cooker: Kuhn Rikon's Duromatic Pressure/Risotto Cooker

$160

The Mercedes Benz of pressure cookers, this 4.2-quart stainless steel beauty features an ergonomic handle and a heavy-gauge pan for fast, even cooking.

It includes a recipe book with timesaving meals because the Duromatic, like other pressure cookers, can cut conventional cooking times up to 70 percent. In fact, risotto, a popular and time-consuming Italian rice-pasta dish, can be prepared in the Duromatic in just 7 minutes. Now that's cooking with speed.

T-Fal's Country Cabin Chicken

(Serves 4)

EQUIPMENT NEEDED: pressure cooker, chef's knife
PREPARATION TIME: an amazing 15 minutes

INGREDIENTS
- 1 medium onion
- 1 stalk celery
- 1 green pepper
- 1 clove garlic
- 1 tsp. olive oil
- 2 tsp. curry powder
- one 20-ounce can whole tomatoes in juice
- ⅓ cup raisins
- 8 skinless chicken thighs (about 2 lbs.)

PREPARATION
- Chop onion, slice celery, and cut the green pepper into 1-inch slices.
- Mince garlic.
- Put olive oil in pressure cooker and cook over medium heat until hot.
- Add onion, celery, pepper, garlic, and curry powder and cook, uncovered, stirring for 2 minutes.
- Add tomatoes with juice, breaking up tomatoes with wooden spoon.
- Stir in raisins and salt to taste.
- Add chicken, making sure all chicken is covered with sauce.
- Cover seal and bring to full pressure.
- Cook for 9 minutes.
- Release pressure with quick-release method. Serve with rice.

Stop the Presses Pressure Cooker: Salton's Electric Pressure Cooker

$200

Talk about last-minute! As this book was being put to bed in the halls of Warner Books, Salton suddenly introduced the world's first electric pressure cooker. This countertop gem eliminates the need to watch over the stovetop during pressure-cooking. That's because it has its own computer chip memory system, which automates everything.

This product will definitely be a hot commodity.

Best Turkey Tamer: The Auto Chef

$140

When it comes to planning a big meal—the kind that consists of a turkey or a roast—time is not exactly on your side. Not only does this type of fare require hours in the oven, the cook must stand watch, periodically basting the dish. But the new Auto Chef Roasting Pan promises to change all that. The Auto Chef is the world's only self-basting roasting pan that uses science (are we beginning to see a trend here?) to automate this chore. Here's how it works.

Simply place the beef or bird into the Auto Chef pan. As the temperature rises, juices drip to the bottom of the pan. But instead of collecting there, they pass through a special valve. Using a technique similar to that of a coffee percolator, the unit draws the juices through two tubes and up onto a grid plate that rests above the bird or meat. Tiny holes in the plate then allow the juices to drip slowly back down, basting the food without any human intervention.

Near the end of the cooking cycle, a flick of a switch blocks the tubes, enabling you to brown the entrée to perfection. Even better, the fact that you don't have to keep opening the oven door means that less heat escapes and your food cooks faster. The manufacturer claims that a 23-pound turkey will cook in 3½ hours, rather than the 6 hours it would take in a standard roasting pan.

TEN STEPS TO A PICTURE-PERFECT TURKEY

Every year, the Butterball Test Kitchen staff roasts countless turkeys to determine the method that will produce the best-tasting, most picture-perfect turkey. Time and again, the Butterball Open Pan Roasting Method wins hands down. This method virtually guarantees a moist, flavorful, golden turkey. Follow these 10 easy steps to create a picture-perfect turkey:

1. If turkey is frozen, thaw in the refrigerator or cold water. When ready to cook, remove the wrapper. Preheat the oven to 325 degrees F.
2. Remove the neck from the body cavity and the giblets from the neck cavity. Drain the juices, and blot the cavities with paper towels.
3. Just before roasting, stuff the neck and body cavities lightly, if desired. Turn the wings back to hold the neck skin in place. Return legs to tucked position, if untucked. No trussing is necessary.
4. Place the turkey, breast side up, on a flat rock in an open roasting pan about 2 inches deep. A handy Turkey Lifter comes with each Butterball turkey. Place this special string cradle on a rack; then place the turkey on top and bring the loops up around the turkey. Do this before putting the turkey in the oven. When it is time to lift the cooked turkey from the pan, use the loops as handles.
5. Insert an oven-safe meat thermometer deep into the lower part of the thigh next to the body, not touching the bone.
6. Brush the skin with vegetable oil to prevent skin from drying. Further basting is unnecessary.
7. Wash preparation utensils, work surfaces, and hands in hot, soapy water following contact with uncooked turkey and juices.
8. Roast at 325 degrees F. For approximate cooking times, figure about 15 minutes per pound of turkey. When the skin is light golden, about two-thirds done, shield the breast loosely with light-weight foil to prevent overcooking.
9. Check for doneness ½ hour before turkey is expected to be done. Turkey is fully cooked when the thigh's internal temperature is 180 degrees F. The thickest part of the breast should read 170 degrees F., and the center of the stuffing should be 160 degrees F.
10. When turkey is done, let it stand for 15 to 20 minutes before carving.

Max Burton Stovetop Smoker

$50

Smoking meats, fish, veggies, even cheese on your stovetop without setting off the fire alarm is easy with this unique device from Max Burton.

Featuring a stainless steel roasting pan with an airtight locking lid, the smoker includes a grill grate and wood chips for smoking. To use, simply add presoaked wood chips, place the grate in the pan, and then put your food on top of the grate. Slide and lock the lid and place it on your cooktop or in the oven. While meats cook in 20 to 30 minutes, fish can be prepared in only 12 minutes. It truly delivers a restaurant-quality flavor to your kitchen.

The World's Smartest Top: The Intelligent Lid

$10–$20

How many times have your favorite sauces boiled over, spilling out on your cooktop before you could rush over and reduce the heat? If you're like me, more times than you want to remember.

To the rescue comes the Intelligent Lid. This cookware replacement lid has a sensor built in to its top that automatically releases steam when pressure is sensed, forever ending the spilled-over syndrome.

Intelligent Lids come in 8-, 10-, and 12-inch lid sizes. An intelligent choice, I must say.

CHAPTER 3

Gimme da Cord

Countertop Appliances

Coffeemakers, food processors, stand mixers, blenders, choppers, toasters, microwaves, bread machines, waffle irons, sandwich makers, indoor grills, slow cookers, pizza makers—they're coming to take me away, ha ha, ho ho, hee hee!

Just wading through the vast quantity of countertop appliances is enough to drive you crazy! There are so many different varieties of countertop appliances, all promising to simplify your cooking chores, that you can truly go batty attempting to select just the right assortment for your lifestyle. Not to mention that you'd need a countertop the size of Texas to house all these items and a fuse box the size of Seattle to power them.

But countertop appliances can help add variety to your menus and, most importantly, assist you in the numerous steps associated with food preparation. The question most asked of us here at the Gadget Guru is: "I've got this great new superpowered appliance, but what can I make with it?" Sure, a stand mixer can help you prepare a triple-layer chocolate mousse cake with sherry-nut icing, but how many of us are really going to attempt a recipe of that magnitude? What most of us want are tools that simplify everyday cooking—products that not only make our lives easier, but are fun and simple to operate.

When you shop, instead of being too impulsive, be sure to ask yourself, "Can this device save me money on prepackaged goods and help shave time off my already hectic schedule?" "Will I use it at least somewhat regularly?" "Can I justify the purchase of an appliance that will occupy valuable counter and storage space if I only plan to use it occasionally?" And (this is the really important question): "How easy is it to clean?"

This chapter will assist you in differentiating fact from fiction and help you understand the features and functions of specific products, as well as the uses and applications of numerous countertop appliances in a vast array of categories. We have polled our multitalented friends and family members and have included a few easy-to-prepare recipes that are so simple, anyone (including you) can prepare them even if you are not a seasoned chef. After all, isn't that what a good countertop appliance is supposed to do—make you look like you really know what you are doing in the kitchen?!

So let's get plugged in and see what we can stir up.

SECTION I

Perk Me Up

Coffee, Espresso, Tea, and Hot Chocolate Makers

Legend has it that around 850 A.D. an Ethiopian goatherd named Kaldi saw his goats behaving a bit nervously after chewing berries from what was then an unknown plant. Even stranger, one goat took to reciting poetry (I just repeat the stories; I don't make them up) while the others began altering their facial hairs and calling them goatees. It wasn't long thereafter that insomniac goatherds appeared all over Africa. Hence, the coffee bean was born.

So tomorrow morning when you stumble out of bed and into the kitchen for a hot, steamy cup of Joe, remember to say a word of thanks to Kaldi's Ethiopian jumping goats for helping you jumpstart your morning.

Here at the Gadget Guru we have our own Kaldi (or goat boy)—coauthor and coffee aficionado John Kelley. While he doesn't have any goats roaming around his palatial estate (that we know of), he has willingly tested every coffeemaker and espresso machine that comes through this joint. And believe me, that alone is a full-time job. John both starts and ends his day with a cup of coffee—and has a few cups in between. Maybe that's why he is able to peruse the trade shows with the speed of Superman. Although he swears he has no other vices, with the possible exception of Juan Valdez, he knows more about coffeemakers than anyone else on the planet.

Whether you're an aficionado like John, or a one-cup-a-day drinker like me, we promise that this section will help you find just the right coffeemaker for your lifestyle. Also included are a vast assortment of espresso machines and a host of nifty gadgets every coffee lover will love.

Although today's coffeemakers are loaded with features that promise great taste and simplify preparation, the one feature that has truly changed the face of coffeemakers is the automatic timer. Before this innovation, we found ourselves attempting to separate the thin paper filters, losing count while loading scoop after scoop of grinds, and fumbling with the water reservoir while we were still in a sleepy state. Today, though, the timer mechanism allows us to preset the coffeemaker before bed and awake to the aroma of freshly ground coffee. If you demand a cup of coffee the FIRST thing in the morning, this feature is too good to pass up, and it's worth a few extra dollars.

Another noteworthy option is the automatic shutoff mechanism. These devices automatically turn off the warming plate after a pre-determined period—usually around two hours. This way, you'll never be driving to work or heading toward the airport wondering, "Did I remember to turn the coffeemaker off?" Definitely a feature that delivers peace of mind.

True coffee junkies will also want a model with automatic drip stop. This feature, which can be called by a variety of trademarked names, allows you to remove the pot in order to sneak a cup while the unit is in the midst of the brewing cycle. You should remember to replace the pot immediately, or you may end up with a mess when the water overflows the grinds.

MORSEL OF KNOWLEDGE

The most expensive coffee in the world comes from Indonesia, where a finicky, raccoonlike marsupial called the palm civet lives on coffee plantations and dines only on the choicest coffee berries. Unlike other pests, however, the palm civet is a welcome intruder. That's because when the palm civet, let's just say . . . adheres to the call of nature, he leaves behind a mound of undigested choice coffee beans. These beans, known to coffee aficionados as Kopi Luwak, are said to make the best pot (pun intended) of brew and are worth their weight in gold. A pound of Kopi Luwak sells for $170. Maybe John Kelley would opt for this variety, but I think I'll stay with the brands that come in a vacuum-packed can.

Best New Brew Coffeemaker: Capresso's Aroma Classic

$160

Although not yet a household name (if my predictions are correct, it soon will be), Capresso is the coffeemaker company to watch. Over the past few years this team of experts has continued to introduce new models that excel above the rest, both in design and in functionality. While last year's hot model was its CoffeeTeam (see page 68), this year it's the Aroma Classic.

Drip coffeemakers have become the standard for home use. They perform well and are relatively simple to set up and use. However, there are a number of other brewing techniques, such as French press, that make what we feel is better-tasting coffee than drip models. Although not as easy to set up, operate, and clean as most drip coffeemakers, some of these alternative devices deliver a restaurant-quality brew to the comfort of your kitchen table. The problem is that most of these methods require a multistep process to prepare—something that most of us don't want to undertake the first thing in the morning. Some require you to boil water on the stove and perform other time-consuming and somewhat complicated steps that just don't make sense for the everyday coffee drinker.

That's what I like about the Aroma Classic—it delivers a French press–like taste and is as easy to use as a drip coffeemaker.

This 8-cup coffeemaker not only delivers a great taste, it is also very pleasing to the eye and will most definitely capture the admiration of your guests. That's because the Aroma Classic looks more like a highly styled device you'd find in the Museum of Modern Art than something that you'd see resting on the shelves of your favorite department store. The Aroma Classic is the first to automate a preferred brewing method (à la the French press), in which the water is boiled in a top glass chamber, then released, via a heat sensitive valve, all at once onto the grounds below. This method allows the water to contact the grounds more quickly than automatic drip coffeemakers and to brew it hotter, for terrific-tasting coffee. The bottom line is that it delivers a great-tasting pot of coffee.

Other features include a unique detachable cord, and a top-mounted carrying handle, which allows you to carry this stylish hourglass-shaped coffeemaker to the table when you entertain. Even better, its hot plate keeps coffee hot for an extra 20 minutes after it is unplugged, without burning its contents.

It has an auto-shutoff mechanism and a stop-and-serve feature, and it comes with a gold-tone reusable filter. However, there is one feature missing—the automatic timer. Maybe next year the folks at Capresso will add that feature to this unit. Also, since the unit is approximately 20 inches tall, it will not fit on the counter underneath most kitchen cabinets, as standard cabinet height is 18 inches. However, those with kitchen "islands" will definitely love the style of this unit, whose footprint is smaller than most. It is definitely a conversation piece.

Best Coffeemaker Marriage: Toastmaster/Porsche Designed Coffeemaker

$200

Speaking of conversation pieces, this model is definitely something to talk about. Understanding that speed and coffee go together like cream and sugar—nobody wants to wait for that first cup of the day—engineers from the fastest carmaker naturally shifted gears and teamed up with a well-known houseware manufacturer to create the Toastmaster/Porsche Designed Coffeemaker. No, you won't need leather driving gloves to operate this unit, but just wait until you see it in person, because, like its four-wheeled counterpart, it looks fast even when it's sitting in neutral.

This sleek, 8-cup coffeemaker features a brushed-aluminum exterior with black accents that will jazz up even the most mundane of kitchens. It features a removable water reservoir with cup measurement markings that you can fill at the sink and insert in the unit—no sloppy pouring required. When the machine is activated, the water automatically transfers from the reservoir to the grounds and into its matching brushed-aluminum insulated pot, which not only keeps the coffee warmer longer than glass pots, it also promises not to crack when it accidentally taps the side walls of your porcelain sink. It also includes a 2- to 4-cup control that alters the brewing technique to deliver a great-tasting small pot.

Trust me; just the appearance alone will make you want to place it on the countertop—whether or not you are a coffee drinker.

Best Art Deco Coffeemaker:
Krups Premium Model No. 253-45

$130

I know that I am beginning to sound like a broken record, but this model not only looks good, it delivers a great-tasting pot of coffee. Like the Capresso Aroma Classic and the Toastmaster/Porsche model, this silver-and-black model is also high on styling. (Are we beginning to see a trend here?) What separates this model from the pack is that its glass carafe features a unique lid that allows it to keep the coffee warmer longer than other glass carafe models. The carafe itself is noteworthy, as it is styled taller than most standard issue coffeemaker carafes. Another notable feature is its deep-brew V-shaped gold cone filter that makes one of the best-tasting automatic pots of brewed coffee that we've found.

Because of its 1- to 3-cup adjustable brewing cycle, you have the option of brewing a small or large pot of coffee. Other features include auto-shutoff and stop-and-serve for instant gratification.

Best Value 12-Cup Coffeemaker: Braun FlavorSelect

$100

For years, Braun has been a leader in upscale coffeemakers. They attempt to stay on top of the game by periodically introducing new models that are not only functional, but include an element of design that definitely captures the eye. Although their Flavor Select model is not new this year, its colors are. And boy, are they different. They feature colors that you'd never expect to see on a coffeemaker.

In terms of function, what separates this coffeemaker from the pack is its self-monitoring water filter, which helps purify the water while you brew. The palm-sized filter snaps into the coffeemaker's water reservoir and features a date-indicator switch that reminds you when it's time to replace it (replacements sell for $5). Each filter lasts for approximately 70 brew cycles (depending on the quality of the water in your area) and removes bitter-tasting chlorine from your water for a better-tasting cup of Joe.

On the styling front, Braun is offering the Flavor Select in new colors: green, blue, and yellow—but not your typical green, blue, and yellow. The green is a bit brighter than a military shade, the blue is cobalt colored, and the yellow . . . well, it reminds me of a New York taxi. So if you're looking for a bold statement for your countertop, this could be just what you are looking for. Other features include automatic settings, auto-shutoff, stop-and-serve, and a digital clock/timer mechanism.

As an accessory, Braun is also offering a companion bean grinder coordinated to each of the three aforementioned colors. They plug in for power and sell for $20.

Coffeemakers with Built-in Grinders: Capresso's CoffeeTeam and Cuisinart's Automatic Grind and Brew

$230 (Capresso), $175 (Cuisinart)

For serious coffee drinkers who don't mind spending a little more for the freshest cup of Java available, both Capresso and Cuisinart offer excellent coffeemakers with built-in grinders.

It doesn't take a rocket scientist to realize that the best cup of coffee starts with the freshest coffee beans. The best way to get restaurant taste at home is to grind the beans just prior to brewing. Yes, you can purchase a separate device to accomplish this task—or you can save a step and take the easy route and buy a coffeemaker with a built-in grinder. They are typically a bit more expensive, and it can take some practice to learn how to use them, but they eliminate the need to transfer the grinds from the grinder to the coffeemaker, and they deliver a superlative taste.

Last year, both John and I selected these units as two of the best of the year—and they still are. However, there are some differences between the two.

To operate the Cuisinart, you start by filling its bean hopper with 1 tablespoon of beans for each cup of coffee desired; it can grind and brew from 4 to 10 cups of coffee. You then set its selector for the amount of cups, and it's ready to go. After that, the machine does all the rest. It grinds the beans, passes them on to the filter, and starts the brewing process. To ensure the best flavor, its settings automatically regulate the amount of water passed directly onto or around the beans. This results in a full-bodied taste. Also included is a cleaning indicator that notifies you when it's time to decalcify the coffeemaker. After you put in a mixture of vinegar and water, it cleans the critical parts in a one-step method. Other features include a strength selector, automatic shutoff, automatic drip stop, and a large, easy-to-set LCD clock.

Although the Capresso unit is more expensive, it has a larger (12-cup) capacity, and it includes a bean storage hopper so that you can pour the beans in and set the coffeemaker for the desired amount of cups as well as preferred strength. It then automatically takes the proper amount of beans, grinds them, and passes them into the filter area. This means no measuring. Its grinder is a Swiss Burr Mill—the most durable and desirable on the market.

However, the Capresso unit does have more moving parts (meaning more could go wrong). Its filter mechanism automatically swings shut when the beans are ground inside and the brewing process begins. This, however, is a sight to be seen; when it moves, it looks like something from the Jetsons' kitchen. In testing, however, it performed with flying colors. Other features include an automatic shutoff mechanism, automatic drip stop, and a large, easy-to-set LCD clock/timer.

**Best Carafe-Style Coffeemaker:
Black & Decker KitchenTools
Model No. TCMKT800**

$170

There are two reasons I like coffeemakers that brew directly into a thermal carafe. The first is that since there is an absence of a warming tray, the thermal characteristics of the carafe keep the coffee at an even temperature without burning. This is an important feature for those who brew a full pot and pour from it over many hours. The second is that since it has a tougher exterior, it is not prone to as much accidental breakage as its glass counterparts. Granted, the insides of most thermal carafes are glass, but they will most likely stay intact—when you accidentally bump them on the sides of the sink, but not if you drop them on a hard floor. This model from Black & Decker is one of my favorite thermal carafe units.

Its carafe features a sleek stainless steel exterior with a push-to-pour lid that seals in the flavor and the heat for hours after brewing. Best of all, you can take your coffee anywhere—from the kitchen to the table to the home office, as the carafe keeps your Java hot for up to five hours. Other features include a gold-tone filter, digital clock timer, and automatic shutoff after each brewing cycle. If you've never used a thermal unit, you may want to give it a try.

Best Coffeemaker for Light Drinkers: KitchenAid's 4-cup Coffeemaker

$40

Many folks, myself included, only drink one or two cups of coffee per day—so brewing a full 8- or 10-cup pot is a waste. For those of us who fit in this category, our choices are to use instant coffee or only brewing a partial pot of coffee. The problem is that both of these techniques usually don't deliver as great-tasting a cup of coffee as you would typically get from a full pot. Yes, instant is convenient, but not that great-tasting. Also, most coffeemakers usually only deliver the best-tasting pots when brewed to capacity. Granted, some higher-end coffeemakers have a switch that allows you to brew smaller portions with great taste but a better alternative for us smaller drinkers is a smaller coffeemaker—that's what I like about this 4-cup coffeemaker from KitchenAid. It is also important to note that smaller-capacity coffeemakers are indeed smaller and take up less counter space.

What separates this coffeemaker from the pack is its hot water brewing technique. With most coffeemakers the first shot of water to hit the grounds is usually not hot enough to brew coffee. With an 8- to 10-cup unit this is not as important as the temperature balances during the brewing cycle, but the smaller coffeemakers (like those pitiful ones found in motel bathrooms) cannot properly brew hot coffee. KitchenAid has changed my perception of smaller-capacity coffeemakers by developing a unit that heats the first shot of water at full temperature so your coffee not only brews properly, but also it's hot when you drink it. So now even the lightest coffee drinker (like me) can enjoy a full rich brew without wasting half a pot a day.

Best Travel Coffeemaker:
Melitta's 1-Cup Coffeemaker

$20

A woman named Melitta Bentz (hence the name Melitta for filters and drip coffeemakers) invented the coffee filter in 1908, freeing millions of coffee lovers from the grind of cloudy and gritty coffee. This led to the first drip coffeemaker and a whole new way to enjoy the black gold.

Giving new meaning to "brew and go," this portable coffeemaker from Melitta features a removable cone filter attachment that brews directly into a 14-ounce insulated stainless steel mug with spillproof lid. To operate, fold #2 filters into the cone attachment, place the cone over the top of the mug, load in fresh coffee, and pour hot water. It's that easy.

ESPRESSO MAKERS

While espresso and cappuccino machines are popular in Europe, gourmet coffee shops, and restaurants, they are in fewer than 10 percent of American homes.

Why? One reason is that making espresso can be a messy and time-consuming task. Another reason is that these machines take up valuable countertop space reserved for more important items like toasters, coffeemakers, food processors, and microwaves. Although you may pull out the espresso maker when you entertain, it most likely will be spending the vast majority of its life gathering dust in the bottom of the pantry or closet.

But this hasn't stopped manufacturers from introducing a slew of new models. The good news is that companies are coming up with unique ways to automate the espresso preparation process. The most promising of these new methods is the introduction of espresso pods. About the size of a silver dollar, these premeasured and pre-ground single-use pods are sealed in a filterlike material for easy preparation and disposal. The pods eliminate the grinding, tamping, and cleaning steps involved with most machines. They also eliminate inaccurate measurements, and definitely are a lot less messy.

For the record, there are two types of espresso machines: steam and pump. While both use steam and pressure to boil water to send through the grounds, pump-based machines have coils inside that help produce three times the pressure of steam-only machines. For that reason steam machines are less expensive, and pump machines typically deliver a fuller, richer taste.

World's First Microwavable Espresso Maker: Expresso Mio Kit from Black & Decker

$25

Before you think we've lost our minds, or our dictionary: We did not misspell the name of this product. In an attempt to have its name look fast—as in "express"—it is called the Expresso Mio, not the Espresso Mio. So blame them, not us!

If you are in a hurry, check out this new espresso kit from Black & Decker. It prepares a double shot of espresso in your microwave in less than two minutes. Featuring a cylinder-shaped container with cool-touch handle and body, it makes two espressos at a time. It's easy to use too. Simply pour water into the unit, add espresso grounds, pop it in the microwave, and in two minutes you're done.

The kit includes the microwave espresso maker, a measuring spoon, and a recipe booklet complete with unique cappuccino recipes from our friend, author and gourmet expert Tom Lacalamita, as well as an easy pump-based instant frother for cream.

Instant Espresso Machine: Salton 1,2,3,-Spresso

$230

If you are looking for the easiest method of making espresso or cappuccino at home, look no further than Salton's 1,2,3,-Spresso. Using pod technology, this unit makes preparing espressos, cappuccinos, and lattes easier than ever. Just add water and drop a premeasured espresso pod piggy bank–style in the top of the unit, place a cup under its spout, and press Brew. It brews one or two shots per pod, and, even better, the biodegradable pods go into a unique chamber for easy disposal. It's really that simple!

The 1,2,3,-Spresso includes a 48-ounce removable water reservoir that makes 40 continuous shots without a refill and features a frothing wand for steaming milk when you make cappuccinos and lattes. It comes with 50 espresso pods (refills sell for $5 per 50) and has a unique cup warmer on its top that keeps your tiny espresso cups warm.

Best Company to Enter the Home Espresso Business: Starbucks Barista

$299

Okay, they're the McDonalds of gourmet coffee, but the one thing you can say about Starbucks is that no matter which store you visit, you can count on the same high-quality cup of Joe. Now Starbucks is expanding its presence from the street-corner and airport kiosk and moving into your kitchen. Not only has it introduced the new Barista espresso machine, it is now selling Starbucks-branded pods. This machine can also accept ground espresso beans.

This stylish unit has a giant 96-ounce removable water reservoir and dispenses one or two shots of espresso at a time into its included shot glasses (like those seen at Starbucks stores). It has a frother rod for making cappuccinos and lattes and comes with 50 pods—replacements sell for $10 for 16 pods.

Espresso on Ice: Cuisinart Iced Cappuccino Maker

$100

Cuisinart has become one of our favorite companies. That's because, unlike many other companies, it doesn't rest on its laurels and take the safe side when introducing new products. It seems that more and more often, Cuisinart is experimenting with new products by intro-ducing new categories, not just new gadgets. This is the case with its Iced Cappuccino Maker.

This unique contraption prepares four 8-ounce iced cappuccinos in less than 5 minutes. To operate, just fill the plastic pot with ice cubes, add espresso in the grounds holder, pour water in one reservoir and a little milk in the other, and press Brew. The machine automatically tamps the espresso, brews it, and warms the milk, delivering it to the pot. You then stir and serve. If you prefer a little heat, the unit also makes 8 hot 1½-ounce espressos per water refill. But the best aspects of this unit are that it is easy to use, relatively easy to clean, and delivers a full, rich taste. Definitely a great pick for the dog days of summer.

Best Hot Tea Maker: Cuisinart Perfect Tea Steeper

$60

If tea is your beverage of choice, Cuisinart's electric tea steeper makes up to eight 5-ounce cups of probably the best-tasting hot tea you've ever consumed, in about 9 minutes. Even better, it allows you to use either loose leaves or bags.

Unlike other tea-brewing devices on the market that use a dripping process, this Cuisinart model uses a steeping (or percolating) process to brew the freshest tea possible. It brings the water to a boil and, depending on the desired strength, steeps the leaves by soaking them in the water for 3 to 5 minutes. The user just presses the On button, and the Tea Steeper does the rest. Not only is this unit easy to use, it truly delivers a brewed tea taste that is noticeably better than tea made by the old-fashioned teabag method.

It also offers a Keep Warm feature that will maintain your tea at 185 degrees F. The carafe has a dripless spout and an ergonomic handle, and it can be removed from the heating base for tabletop serving. It's also attractive, with a high-tech, science experiment–type of look.

Best New Way to Make Hot Chocolate: Mr. Coffee's Cocomotion

$50

There's nothing better than a hot cup of cocoa on a cool winter night. Now the folks at Mr. Coffee have made it easier than ever to prepare your favorite chocolate brew all year round.

The Cocomotion is the world's first hot chocolate maker that simultaneously heats, blends, and aerates its ingredients to make up to four 8-ounce cups of frothy hot chocolate in about 10 minutes. Just add water or milk plus chocolate or powder, and the machine heats your cocoa to 175 degrees F. while it's being mixed. It's machine washable and has no sharp blades, making it safer for the kids to operate as well.

COFFEE ACCESSORIES

Best New Coffee Accessory: SwissMar's AlpenRöst Coffee Bean Roaster

$300

As this company's press release says, "You don't buy your bread toasted, why buy your beans roasted?" Actually, you'd have to be a pretty serious coffee drinker to want a bean roaster, but believe me, there is a huge market out there.

Looking like a mini airplane engine, this unit roasts ½ pound of green coffee beans in about 15 to 20 minutes. What's better is that green beans traditionally cost about 50 percent less than roasted beans, so you can attempt to justify the cost of the machine right off the bat. Not only does it roast the green beans to perfection, it automatically shucks the shells and places them in a holding area for easy disposal. This unit is dishwasher safe too.

Best Coffee Mate: KitchenArt T'spooner

$13

This is a handheld, spice jar–like container that holds up to 5 ounces of your favorite powdered substance. A squeeze of its side-mounted lever delivers exactly ½ teaspoon of sugar, nondairy creamer, or any powdered substance directly into your cup. Not just good for coffee additives, it's ideal for spices as well. It also includes a shaker top that allows you to sprinkle its contents and a cover to prevent moisture from ruining the contents.

Best Bean Grinder: Bodum Antigua

$100

If you are looking for a new method of storing and grinding your coffee beans, you'll definitely want to check this one out. This bean grinder not only grinds your beans, it looks great on your countertop too.

Besides its great-looking high-tech aesthetics, what really separates Bodum's Antigua from the pack is its bean hopper and precision grinding capabilities. Its top-mounted bean hopper provides an airtight holding area for up to 1 pound of beans, making it an ideal storage place for your favorite bag of beans. It has a two-step grinding gear that prevents accidental heating of the beans (which can harm the flavor), and 8 grind settings ranging from fine Espresso to coarse French Press. For more accurate measurements, the Antigua includes a time-controlled switch that allows the user to dial the specific number of cups desired (between 1 and 12), and grinds until the proper time has elapsed.

SECTION II

Bread Winners

Toasters, Toaster Ovens, and Bread Machines

The toaster is the Rodney Dangerfield of kitchen appliances. To prove it, strike up a conversation at your next dinner party about the wonders of the pop-up toaster and see how fast you clear the room. Compared to a sexy food processor or stand mixer, or a cool new coffeemaker, the toaster gets no respect at all—but it is a necessity and has passed the test of time. In fact, the toaster is like the telephone—you plug it in, it works, and it's so easy to use that you take it for granted and forget it's there. Because it's typically used on a daily basis, you keep it on the countertop and rarely, if ever, hide it away in the back of a closet. If you ask me, that's the definition of the ultimate gadget—something so sophisticated, yet simple and useful, that we hardly notice it.

This section will examine the bread winners of the kitchen: the best toasters, toaster ovens, and bread machines, all of which deliver the goods without taking all your dough. So if you "knead" one of these units, rest assured you're not loafing around by reading this section.

Best Bagel Toaster: Toastmaster Bagel Perfect Toaster

$69

After years of testing toasters that claim to toast bagels properly, I have encountered a problem: Although most new toasters feature wider slots that promise to be ideal for bagels, they really are not.

That's because they toast both sides of the bagel simultaneously. That's not the way it should be done.

For a cut bagel to be properly toasted, it should be toasted on the face side and merely heated on the outside, not toasted on both sides. This way you don't burn your hands while trying to eat it. Although Bryant Gumbel literally "toasted" me on the air when I explained my theory, I am sticking to my guns and saying that this is indeed the proper way to toast a bagel. I have finally located a toaster that performs this task properly: Toastmaster's Bagel Perfect Toaster.

This unit has a nifty Bagel switch that toasts two halves simultaneously. To use, just turn the switch to the Bagel mode and place the bagel halves in the slot with the cut side facing the center of the toaster.

The heating elements toast at two different temperature settings. While the inside elements are hot enough to toast evenly, the outside elements only warm—making for a perfectly toasted bagel. (This feature is also ideal for English muffins.) Even better, after each toasting cycle, the switch automatically returns to its standard Bread Mode so that you don't accidentally half-toast the next slice of bread. Also available is a 6-slice unit for $100.

Best Multislice Toaster: Kenmore 4-Slice Toaster Model No. 48339

$45

The sleek rounded-style 4-slice toaster features four extralong and -wide slots for a variety of breads, and a built-in computer chip that can sense the thickness of the bread to toast it accordingly.

Another unique feature is its Frozen Bread button, which allows you to defrost and toast with the press of one button. It has an easy pull-out crumb tray, an extra lift lever for smaller breads (so you won't think about putting in a knife to retrieve your toast), and a cool-touch body with a safety cutoff control as well.

TOASTER OVENS

A staple in dorm rooms and efficiency apartments across the land, today's toaster ovens will not only brown your bread, some will cook whole meals like roasts, pizzas, and hors d'oeuvres. In fact, if you have a lot of mouths to feed at breakfasttime, a toaster oven could be just the ticket; it's the short-order chef of the kitchen. One warning, though: If you are planning to use a toaster to heat frozen entrées, be sure to read the manufacturers' preparation instructions. Some manufacturers do not recommend heating in a toaster oven or may give a different time or temperature setting.

Best 6-Slice Toaster Oven: Oster Toast Logic

$100

It's not brain surgery, but Oster's Toast Logic technology is actually pretty cool. It incorporates a computer chip, which guarantees that your toast will come out the way you like it, time after time. That's because its internal electronics prevent power surges and other electrical interruptions from interfering with toaster operations. So take that, El Niño!

Oster's oven features a pull-down glass door and a whopping .4 cubic feet of cooking area—enough room for a small roast or chicken, or for broiling meat and fish. Other features include a 60-minute timer, an easy-to-remove crumb tray, and a toast lever that operates like one in a pop-up toaster, so you'll feel right at home using this device.

**Best Featured Toaster Oven:
Welbilt's Toaster Oven
with Rotisserie and Griddle
Model No. TBR5**

$139

Whether you have a cramped dorm room or one of those lovely New York City efficiencies, you'll love this multipurpose toaster oven. That's because not only does it have a griddle built in to its top for frying and sautéing, it also has a rotisserie spit attachment inside for roasting chickens up to 5 pounds. Of course, it also toasts up to 6 slices of bread at a time. Other features include wire bake racks, a cookie sheet insert, a drip pan, and an easy-to-clean crumb tray. It can even prepare cakes and pies up to 9 inches in diameter.

It has a temperature dial that heats up to 480 degrees F. and a function selector dial to choose from Broil, Rotisserie, Toast, or Bake.

BREAD MACHINES

Automatic bread machines give new meaning to "loafing" around the kitchen. That's because they have become the easiest way ever to bake a loaf of just about any type of bread.

These units first surfaced on the market more than a decade ago and have steadily risen in sales. One reason for the bread machine's popularity is its ease of use. To bake a fresh loaf of bread, just pour the ingredients into its baking pan and press Start. A few hours later, the bread is ready—it's really that simple. This way, even rookies can impress their friends by adding freshly baked bread to the fare.

Making things even easier, numerous companies have introduced prepackaged bread mixes, requiring only the addition of water and/or milk to complete the recipe. Prepackaged mixes can be found in grocery, gourmet, and department stores for $2 to $3.

Today's bread machines range in price from $99 for basic units to $350 for full-featured, larger-capacity machines.

Another benefit to bread machines is the wonderful aroma they emit while the bread is baking. It's almost worth the price of buying a bread machine to have your house smell like a fresh bakery, even if you don't like the bread. Even better, most units have timers and can be set up at night, so you can wake up the next morning to that fresh bread flavor—definitely a great way to start the day.

Best Value Bread Machine: Welbilt Bakers' Select

$130

Taking the bread machine to new heights is Welbilt, with its new Bakers' Select unit. What separates this unit from the pack is that it automatically ejects the bread after baking. This feature not only prevents your burning your hands on its hot metal cylinder while you try to remove the bread from the pan, it bakes crisper bread, because the moisture is released when the bread is ejected. This machine bakes a 1-, 1½-, or 2-pound loaf and has 5 settings for Basic, Wheat, Rapid Rise, French, and Dough.

Best High-Tech Bread Machine: Salton Dream Machine

$250

Baking bread just went high-tech with this space-age bread machine from Salton. Equipped with a computer chip and a variety of built-in recipes, this unit features, instead of buttons and knobs, a large LCD touch screen for its control functions. To operate, you just press the on-screen buttons, scroll through its memory for the type of bread you wish to prepare, and press the screen. In an instant, your recipe appears on the screen, along with a complete nutritional analysis of the bread. It also automatically alters the baking technique for that specific type of bread. Yes, this is a no-brainer!

It bakes a 1-, 1½-, or 2-pound horizontal loaf of bread and features a 15-hour delay bake timer and power failure backup. This unit has it all—everything except a remote control—but our buddy Barb Westfield, our Salton representative, is working on that.

World's Fastest Bread Machine: Zojirushi Home Bakery Traditional Model BBCC-V20

$250

Many years ago, when I saw my first Zojirushi bread machine, I wondered why someone would introduce into the American market a bread machine with a name that's so difficult to pronounce and spell. Well, Zojirushi did it, and it has done very well with its line of automatic bread machines.

Zojirushi makes some of the best bread machines in the business. Now it's bettered itself with the industry's fastest machine. Instead of the traditional 3 hours and 40 minutes to 4 hours most units take, this speedy unit prepares up to a 2-pound loaf in just 1 hour and 50 minutes. How? The unit is equipped with two kneading blades instead of one, which makes mincemeat out of baking times. In addition, it bakes the bread in a more loaflike horizontal position, as opposed to the more common vertical machine.

But we aren't through yet. Other features include 10 baking cycles, including Whole Wheat, and a Homemade Menu that lets you enter your favorite custom bread recipes into its memory for easy retrieval.

The machine also has a 13-hour programmable timer for automatic cooking, a large viewing window, and an automatic shutoff feature for safety. Okay, we're done; you may now proceed to the next section.

SECTION III

Chop Till You Drop

Food Processors, Choppers, Mixers, and Blenders

Devices that chop things in the kitchen fascinate not only cooks, but comedians too. I mean, who could forget Dan Aykroyd's Bass-a-Matic or John Belushi's Samurai Chef (both from the early days of *Saturday Night Live*) or for that matter the real products that inspired them: the Mouli, the Veg-a-matic, and the Ginzu knife?

This section is all about chopping, mixing, and whipping your way to better meals. We'll help you decide if you really need a big food processor or just a little chopper—or both. We'll look at the versatile blender and show how it's not just for margaritas and milkshakes anymore. And for those of you with a sweet tooth, we'll examine hand and stand mixers, giving you some sugary delights from our recipe collection to help you on your way.

FOOD PROCESSORS

Richard Nixon's presidency wasn't the only thing being sliced and diced in 1973. That was also the year that Cuisinart introduced the food processor. (Okay, the first food processor was really the Robot Coup, but that was commercial, not a consumer product.) In fact, it is rumored that a Cuisinart food processor was in the White House kitchen next to the office where the infamous tape recording machines were kept—Oliver Stone, are you listening?

As a testament to its enduring quality and popularity, 26 years later many of us still refer to any food processor as a Cuisinart—it is the generic name of the tool.

The food processor is the workhorse of the kitchen. It consists of a powerful motor, a bowl, and a variety of interchangeable blades and discs that allow you to slice, dice, chop, and mix almost any ingredients with ease and at lightning speed.

MAN VS. MACHINE
IN
SLICE-A-MANIA

Food Processor vs. Human: This is a test I demonstrated on the *Weekend Today* show recently to prove the versatility and speed of a food processor.

Event #1 Grating Cheese

Food Processor: Can grate a whole block of cheese in about two seconds.

Human: A few minutes to accomplish this task.
One bonus point goes to Food Processor for avoiding scraped knuckles.

Score:
Food Processor: 2
Human: 0

Event #2 Slicing Fruits and Vegetables

Food Processor: Carrots, cucumbers, apples, garlic, or onions in just a few seconds each.

Human: Slicing knife, cutting board, bowl at least 3 minutes.
A bonus point goes to the Food Processor for sloppy uneven cuts from human hands—not to mention the unintentional manicure.

Score:
Food Processor: 4
Humans: 0

Event #3 Kneading Dough

Food Processor: 10 minutes

Human: Turning, twisting—oh, the pain! Not to mention the possible injuries and the ensuing mess.

Score:
Food Processor: 5
Humans: 0

Event #4 Cleanup Battle

Food Processor: Detach bowl and blade or cutting disc and place in the dishwasher.

Human: Clean knives, cutting board, and bowl.
They are comparable tasks, but a bonus point awarded to Food Processor for Human's dirty countertop.

Score:
Food Processor: 7
Humans: 0

Event #5 Mike Tyson vs. Food Processor

Okay, one out of five is still not bad, but would you pay to see Tyson in the ring with a food processor? Would you pay to see Tyson in the ring at all?

Final Score:
Food Processor: 7
Humans: 1

➤**Tip:** When you buy a food processor, it's not necessary to buy one with a number of speeds like a blender or stand mixer has. One speed will do most of your work. A Pulse button is a nice additional feature, if not a necessity, since it allows you to chop in quick intervals by simply pressing a button. It also allows you to control the amount of chopping on a specific item.

Best Food Processor: Cuisinart Professional Series
$340

Still the best in the business, this 11-cup food processor can tackle any culinary job. It features a shatterproof, heat- and cold-resistant Lexan bowl and two large feed tubes (instead of one, as on most units) for inserting whole fruits and vegetables.

It comes with 5 blades (a 2 mm slicing disc, a standard 4 mm slicing disc, a medium shredding disc, a dough blade, a metal blade) and a storage container for unused blades. But that's not all; it also includes a helpful how-to video that will get you started in no time.

➤**Tip:** If you purchase a new product that includes a video, take a few minutes to view it. This is a quick and easy method of learning about many of the features of your new product.

Best Feature on a Food Processor: KitchenAid Ultra Power Food Processor with Bowl in Bowl
$200

This product combines an 11-cup food processor with a removable 2-cup chopping bowl/blade that nestles inside the larger bowl for chopping smaller items like garlic and onions. This small bowl is also easier to clean.

Included are a mini bowl with a mini Sabatier blade attachment, a dough blade, a full-sized Sabatier blade, a reversible slicing/shredding disc, a medium shredding disc, and a dual-purpose spatula. Other features include easy-to-use controls (with both Chop and Pulse modes), a membranelike pad for easy cleaning, and a storage box for unused blades.

Fast and Easy Salsa Recipe from Cuisinart

(Serves a party)

EQUIPMENT NEEDED: food processor, chopping knife
PREPARATION TIME: 10 minutes

INGREDIENTS
- ¼ cup fresh cilantro, stems removed
- 2 jalapeño peppers, cut in half lengthwise and seeds removed
- 2 large cloves garlic
- 1 tsp. salt and pepper
- 2 tbs. lime juice
- 4 large vine-ripened tomatoes, each cut into 6 pieces
- 1 medium onion, peeled and cut into 1-inch pieces

PREPARATION
- Place cilantro, garlic, and jalapeño peppers in food processor bowl and process for about 15 seconds.
- Scrape the bowl and add salt, pepper, and lime juice and pulse twice (about 5 seconds).
- Then add tomatoes and onions on top of ingredients in bowl and pulse until they are finely chopped (about 15 seconds).
- Pour the mixture into a serving bowl and serve with tortilla chips and, of course, plenty of ice-cold *cerveza*.

Sunset Grill's Arugula and Walnut Pesto Pasta

(Serves 4)

What's arugula? We don't know, but it sure tastes good—especially in this pasta dish from Randy Rayburn's Sunset Grill Restaurant. Randy suggests you ask your grocer for a batch—it's great in any pasta.

EQUIPMENT NEEDED: food processor
PREPARATION TIME: 15 minutes

INGREDIENTS
- 1 tsp. chopped garlic
- 1 cup toasted walnuts
- 1 tsp. lemon juice
- 2 cups arugula
- 1 cup basil, loosely packed
- ¼ cup grated Parmesan cheese
- ½ cup olive oil
- salt and pepper to taste

PREPARATION
- Combine garlic, walnuts, and lemon juice in a food processor; pulse into a rough paste.
- Add arugula and basil and pulse for about 20 seconds.
- With the processor running, stream in the oil, and season with salt and pepper.
- Toss with your favorite pasta and top with Parmesan cheese.
- Serve with a Sauvignon Blanc.

MINI CHOPPERS

They're not little motorcycles, and to our knowledge Harley-Davidson has not entered the housewares industry. Mini choppers are efficient little versions of the food processor that can handle many of the chopping chores of their larger counterparts. If you don't want or need a big food processor, consider a mini chopper. It'll make your life easier—especially when you are faced with those smaller, tedious chopping chores.

Sunset Grill's Chocolate Pot De Creme

(Serves 12)

The Sunset Grill in Nashville, Tennessee, features new American cuisine and is owned and operated by our good friend, excellent chef, and marginal snow skier Randy Rayburn. The Sunset Grill is the winner of numerous awards for its food and spectacular wine list (who knew there was good vino in Tennessee?); call them up when you're in town at (615) 386-3663. Tell them Guru sent you, and get a 10 percent discount! (Yeah, right!)

EQUIPMENT NEEDED: stand mixer, saucepan, measuring cups, mesh strainer, mixing bowls, and 12 ovenproof ramekins (small baking dishes)
PREPARATION TIME: 30 minutes

INGREDIENTS
- **8 ounces bittersweet chocolate**
- **½ cup sugar**
- **15 egg yolks**
- **1 quart heavy cream**
- **1 vanilla bean**

PREPARATION
- Chop chocolate in food processor, in mini chopper, or by hand.
- In a stand mixer, combine sugar and egg yolks, and whisk until the mixture begins to ribbon.
- In a saucepan scald half the cream over medium heat.
- Split the vanilla bean and scrape the seeds into the cream.
- Pour the warm cream over chocolate in a separate bowl to melt it.
- Pour remaining cream in the stand mixer bowl with the egg yolks, then whisk in the chocolate mixture.
- Strain even portions through a chinois or fine mesh strainer into the 12 ramekins.
- Place the ramekins in a shallow roasting pan and add enough warm water to come halfway up the side of the ramekins.
- Cover with foil and bake at 275 degrees F. for 25–30 minutes until set.
- Allow to cool.
- Serve with a nice tawny port dessert wine.

Best Mini Chopper: Krups Speedy Pro
$30

What separates this little 3-cup chopper from the pack is its 2-ingredient lid, which allows you to mix in oil or mayonnaise while chopping, without removing the top. Its stainless steel blade will easily chop a wide variety of foods, from fresh herbs, vegetables, chocolate, and nuts to hard cheeses. It has a 240-watt motor and hidden cord storage.

Best Chopping Ensemble: Sanyo Cord Free Collection
$100 to $230

Let's face it: Using products with cords in the kitchen can be a tangling experience. That's why cordless products make sense. Included in this offering are a cheese grater, a can opener, a food chopper/mini processor, a coffee mill, a knife sharpener, a hand blender, and a salt-and-pepper mill.

Instead of AC power and unsightly cords, Sanyo's Cord Free collection operates on rechargeable batteries. And to keep the cost low, all appliances share the same battery—really. The cylindrical rechargeable NiCad battery quickly and easily slips in and out of each appliance and into its included charger when not in use. Six hours in the charger bring the battery to full power. Although the charger has slots for two batteries, only one is included. It's a good idea to purchase a second one in case the power runs out before a job is completed. If not, don't worry; you can always pick up the phone and order a pizza. Additional batteries will sell for $20.

STAND AND HAND MIXERS

If you bake a lot of cakes, cookies, bread, quiches, and pies, then you need to consider purchasing a stand or hand mixer. These handy devices make it easy to beat eggs, mix dough, and aerate liquids at a variety of speeds.

The stand mixer is a big powerful bulky machine used in professional kitchens and by serious home chefs for kneading dough for baking, whipping egg whites for cake batter, and making whipped cream. Unlike food processors, which do not allow much air to enter the bowl, stand mixers give bakers the ability to aerate food and to make fluffier meringues and batters. Hand mixers, on the other hand, are more portable and ideal for smaller jobs. Although it performs most of the functions of a stand mixer, the hand mixer's motor is not as strong as the one in a stand mixer.

➤**Tip:** If you're new to baking, purchase one of the less expensive hand mixers and get some experience before buying a stand mixer. When you're ready to step up, look no further than the KitchenAid stand mixer—simply the best in the business. (See page 93 for details.)

Smartest Hand Mixer: Cuisinart SmartPower

$80

This brainy hand mixer is the world's first that keeps track of your mixing times. How? A built-in digital clock/timer on its handle automatically begins when you squeeze the trigger and stops automatically at the preset time. Yes, no more One Mississippi, two Mississippi, while you're mixing. Just watch the digital display and follow the recipe's directions to the second.

For the messy chef, it also includes a SmoothStart feature that gradually speeds up the beaters to eliminate splattering—trust me, this is a great feature! It has 9 different speeds with 3 extra-low settings, a rotating swivel cord that never gets in the way, and a powerful 220-watt motor that ensures you'll never get bogged down in thick mixes like cookie dough. It comes with two self-cleaning stainless steel beaters and a chef's whisk.

Best Stand Mixer: KitchenAid Professional Stand Mixer Model No. K45SS

$300

What Cuisinart did for the food processor, KitchenAid did for the stand mixer. A staple in any self-respecting baker's kitchen and many smaller restaurants, this stand mixer not only whips, mixes, and purees, it is one of the most versatile appliances on the market today.

What separates the KitchenAid from the pack is its powerful 10-speed motor, its heavy-duty design (it weighs 22 pounds), and its endless list of accessories and attachments, which allow you to do everything from whipping egg whites to kneading dough to stuffing sausages. It includes a 4½-quart stainless steel mixing bowl, a whisk attachment, a dough hook for kneading, and a flat beater.

The best things about the KitchenAid Stand Mixer are all the interchangeable accessories you can add to it. Here's a list:

- Food grinder
- Pasta maker
- Sausage stuffer
- Fruit and vegetable strainer
- Disc slicer shredder
- Rotor slicer shredder
- Grain mill can opener
- Citrus juicer

BLENDERS

Remember your parents' blender? Sure, it looked all shiny and new at first, but after a few months and several daiquiri and margarita parties, it developed strange barnaclelike growths around its keypad. Eventually, the Chop key would cease to be operational and the others followed suit until all that was left was one button that you literally had to jackhammer to get the unit going.

Today the blender is perhaps the most versatile and affordable appliance in the kitchen. No longer do you have to store it just because the summer's over. Blenders are perfect for soups, stocks, and pancake batter, not to mention the old standards: crushed ice, margaritas, daiquiris, and milk shakes. And because of new innovations such as wipe-clean membrane keypads, food will never spill inside the control buttons and make the blender inoperable, or something that looks like it came from an *X-Files* episode.

Best Value Kitchen Blender: Hamilton Beach Blendmaster

$20

Anyone can afford this 7-speed best-value blender. Yes, for $20— that's only $20—you get a powerful 350-watt 7-speed blender with

a stainless steel blade and 40-ounce plastic pitcher. Now that's value.

Don't let its low cost fool you; this unit can chop, crush ice, blend, whip, and grind with the best of them. It also features a handy removable 2-ounce measuring filler cap, which allows you to add ingredients and measure them too. This is the model I keep in my Miami Beach apartment, and I can tell you firsthand that it is ideal for crushing ice for the piña coladas I sip on the balcony while watching the cruise ships sail by.

Bodacious Blender: Cuisinart SmartPower Blender

$120

This stylish 7-speed blender can tackle almost any job in the kitchen. It features a powerful motor and a unique wide-body 40-ounce glass pitcher with an easy-to-pour dripless spout. Even better, it has its own dedicated ice-crushing button for frozen treats. A permeated touch pad makes cleaning a one-swipe operation, and its heavy base keeps the unit from wandering across your countertop.

In addition, this unit eliminates the turning and twisting required for attaching the pitcher. Just press on the base, and that's it. It forms a strong seal and is completely leak resistant. It has a 2-ounce removable measuring lid for adding ingredients and a stainless steel blade.

Uncle Bernie's Potato Latkes

(Serves as many as you need)

Each and every Chanukah, my family gathers at my house not only to celebrate this festival of lights, but also to trade gifts and dine on my brother's famous latkes. For those not familiar, latkes are potato pancakes that in many households are the traditional fare for the first night of Chanukah. Every season, Bernie also takes on the massive project of heading to our Jewish Community Center and preparing enough of these famous latkes to feed the entire local Jewish community. Trust me, they are so good that folks wait in line for hours for a plate full of these delicacies. Bernie didn't actually invent this recipe; he modified it from one that was passed down by our father, Eugene Pargh. Our dad has the knack of taking simple recipes and making them taste great. Be sure to check out his famous Seashells recipe on page 53. But you don't have to wait until Chanukah to try this delicious, albeit filling recipe, as it's easy enough to prepare any time of the year. Serve it with sour cream or applesauce for dipping.

EQUIPMENT NEEDED: blender, skillet
PREPARATION TIME: 20 minutes per batch

INGREDIENTS FOR ONE BATCH
- 2 cups Idaho potatoes, diced
- 1 egg
- 1 cup yellow onions, diced
- ½ cup matzoh meal
- 1 tsp. salt
- 1 tsp. freshly ground black pepper
- peanut oil

PREPARATION
Create small batches in the blender to fry in skillet or on griddle (like pancake mix).
- Hand wash and scrub unpeeled potatoes and dice into ½-inch cubes.
- Place ingredients in blender with egg, onions, potatoes, then dry ingredients. Blend until just mixed. Let sit for five minutes.

The mixture will thicken during this time.

- Put ½ inch oil in large skillet on medium high heat.
- When oil starts to get warm, test a small teaspoon of the mixture. When the batter starts to fry, place large spoon-sized portions in the skillet and fry both sides until golden brown.
- Place on paper grocery bag to drain any excess oil—it works better than paper towels.

Another Awesome Blender: KitchenAid Ultra Power

$140

Like the Cuisinart SmartPower Blender, this blender can take on just about any chopping job in the kitchen. It features a 40-ounce glass pitcher with a quick-lock lid that prevents splashing and a convenient pouring spout that allows you to pour without removing the lid. There's also a separate cap in the center of the lid for adding ingredients.

Other features include a wipe-clean touch control pad with 6 speeds (Stir, Chop, Mix, Puree, Pulse, and Liquefy). It has a stainless steel blade, and its sleek styling will blend right in with your countertop.

SECTION IV

Nuke 'em Duke 'em

Microwaves

Back in the late 1960s, my family was the first on our block to own one of these Jetson-style marvels—an Amana Radarange that could boil a cup of water in about a minute. Just as quickly, it seemed, it became the talk of the neighborhood. Back then, we used it mainly for heating water, reheating food, or making popcorn. But that was before Orville Redenbacher flooded the market with microwave popcorn packages. With our Amana, we took a paper bag, placed a few kernels of popcorn and a tablespoon of butter inside, and placed it in the microwave for a few minutes. One late night, although I knew that the bag was supposed to be tied with string, I couldn't find any, so I used a twist tie instead. I quickly learned, after seeing the sparks and hearing the loud pops, why you were not supposed to place metal objects in a microwave.

Today, microwave ovens have come a long way since that old Amana. In fact, today more than 90 percent of American households own a microwave oven. This market saturation has spawned entire industries ranging from frozen foods to cookware, all designed for microwave ovens. The evolution of the microwave has been equally impressive, with the latest models boasting more features and functionality than ever before.

MORSEL OF KNOWLEDGE

Microwave cooking was discovered in 1946 by Dr. Percy Spencer, a scientist from the Raytheon Company. Spencer accidentally cooked a candy bar in his pocket while standing too close to a magnetron tube he was testing. When he realized he'd been close to the tube when the candy melted, the inevitable lightbulb appeared above his head. Aha! Radiation from the tube must have cooked the candy bar. After changing his pants, Spencer picked up some popcorn kernels from the market, put them near the tube, and voilà! They exploded all over the place. Six years later, consumer microwaves brought about the first new cooking technology in over a million years. It sure beats rubbing two sticks together!

World's Smartest Microwave: Sharp's Multiple Choice Microwave Model No. R390AK

$200

This 1,000-watt oven eliminates the dials and keypads found on most models. Instead it features a unique extralarge interactive LCD screen

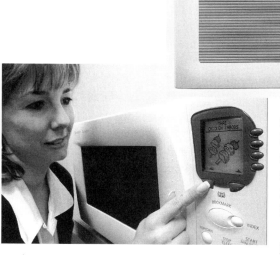

that, at the touch of a button, displays the more than 200 illustrations, 100 recipes, and 80 serving ideas stored in its memory.

To operate, you simply scroll to an item, make your selection from the on-screen menu, and press the Start button; the unit can automatically cook more than 60 food categories. It also has 8 automatic defrost programs and detailed, step-by-step instructions for cooking exotic dishes such as artichokes with mustard sauce, shrimp scampi, and even unique children's recipes like jelly fluffer nut squares. For reheating, the microwave's sensors determine cooking times and power levels. Other features include a child lock, which deactivates the control panel, and a popcorn key with sensor technology for the perfect pop. It has 1 cubic foot of interior space.

Weirdest Microwave Technology: Sanyo's Super Shower Wave Microwave Model EM-P740W

$230

This 1,000-watt microwave features a unique technology called Super Shower Wave. Here's how it works: Instead of having a smooth interior, the oven walls are embossed and have a rough-looking and -feeling texture. When combined with the unit's microwave patterns, it produces a web of evenly distributed microwaves that have the effect of penetrating the food instead of dead air, for more thorough cooking and defrosting. Other features include a Sure Defrost function, which eliminates the frozen spots sometimes left in the middle of some defrosted foods, and seven direct access buttons (Potato, Frozen Vegetables, Popcorn, Soup, Pizza Slice, Frozen Entrée, Roll/Muffin) for automatic cooking.

In addition, its carousel turntable has a unique "boomerang" feature that automatically returns dishes to their original starting point whenever you open the door—so your handles will always be facing outward.

The unit also has a whopping 1.6 cubic feet of interior space.

Children's Microwave Recipe from Sharp: Bananas Snug in a Pancake Blanket

(Serves 1 or 2)

EQUIPMENT NEEDED: microwave, microwavable plates, knife
PREPARATION TIME: 2 minutes

INGREDIENTS
- **2 frozen pancakes**
- **1 tbs. peanut butter**
- **1 tbs. jelly (Hint: Squeezable containers are easier.)**
- **½ banana, peeled and cut in half lengthwise**
- **12 miniature marshmallows**

PREPARATION
- Place both frozen pancakes on a microwavable safe plate. Microwave on High (100%) for 35–45 seconds, or until warm
- Remove, spread each pancake with peanut butter, and top it off with jelly.
- Place one piece of banana cut side up on top of jelly.
- Top each banana with 6 marshmallows and fold pancake up around banana to form a pocket.
- Microwave on high for 20 seconds, or until marshmallows are melted and pancake is heated throughout.
- Serve with a tall glass of milk.

Best New Microwave Technology: Samsung's Dual Cook Microwave Oven Model No. MW6584W

$150

This 1,000-watt microwave is the world's first to cook two separate foods simultaneously at different temperatures and rates. How? Samsung has positioned an elevated rack inside the oven that allows certain items to cook at a faster rate below and a slower rate above. This way your entrée gets most of the power and your side dish located on the elevated rack cooks, but at a lower temperature.

It also features 11 instant-cook touch settings that include a grilling function for browning meats and a special setting for heating baby foods. Other features include 10 power levels, a child safety lock, an automatic defrost function, and a 1.2 cubic foot interior with turntable and built-in rack.

Best Midsize Microwave: Amana Model No. M96T

$160

Although the other models prepare whole meals, many of us just need a microwave to warm foods and prepare smaller items like potatoes, popcorn, or bacon.

This 800-watt oven is a perfect fit. It features 6 programmed touch pads (Popcorn, Beverage, Pizza, Potato, Bacon, Frozen Dinner), a 1-minute touch cook pad, a rotating turntable, auto defrost, and a child lockout. It has 0.9 cubic feet of interior space.

SECTION V

A Cornucopia of Countertop Contraptions

No matter what needs to be prepared in the kitchen, somebody some-where has thought of an easier way to do it. Believe me, here at the Gadget Guru headquarters we've seen everything from hot dog machines, to toasters with stencils that etch out "Good Morning" or "I Love You" on your toast, to blenders with telephones attached to them—really. In fact, the Blender/Phone was such a novelty that I took great pride in showing it on *Late Night with Conan O'Brien* and watching as he demonstrated how you could make a margarita and call your friends at the same time. But don't look for it in stores, as it was just a novelty and really does not have a practical use in the kitchen.

As if you didn't already have a kitchen full of electric gadgets, there are a number of specialty appliances that, depending on your style of cooking, might prove to be just as important as the more tra-ditional guys.

This section will look at Crock-Pots, waffle irons, sandwich mak-ers, and two of the hottest trends in countertop appliances: indoor grills and infusion cookers.

But beware, in the time it takes you to read this section, someone will have reinvented the wheel, and it'll probably be at our doorstep.

SLOW COOKERS

Once the darling of the kitchen, the slow cooker has been nudged off the countertop by sexier new appliances like the food processor and the microwave.

Two words explain its demise: "slow" and "cooker." Who cooks slowly in the kitchen these days? That said, the slow cooker is reportedly still lurking in over 80 percent of American kitchens. Of course it may be being used as a change bowl or flowerpot.

Nevertheless, slow cookers, one of my favorite countertop items, are great for making chili, stews, meats, and beans of all types. They're easy to use too. Just put in your ingredients in the morning before work, turn it on, and the unit will slowly cook your meal all day so that when you get home, dinner is served. Even better, many foods taste noticeably better when prepared in a slow cooker. Meats are more tender and juicy, soups have more flavor—just about anything cooked slowly promises to be the highlight of the meal.

Killer Slow Cooker: West Bend Professional Series 4-QT Slow Cooker

$50

This stylish charcoal gray slow cooker features a nonstick coated interior with adjustable temperature controls, stainless steel handles, and a see-through glass top.

This model looks so good, it may shove the food processor back in the closet and take center stage.

Best Idea Slow Cooker: Sunbeam Automatic Slow Cooker

$38

While slow cookers deliver meals that you don't have to constantly watch over, until now, you still had to stir the stuff inside every now and then. Enter the Sunbeam self-stirring slow cooker. It does everything but eat your soup, stew, or chili for you. Located inside its cooking well is a stirring blade that slowly stirs your ingredients while cooking. Even better, if the rotating blade gets stuck on one of your famous meatballs, no worry; it automatically reverses itself.

Available in a 4- or 6-quart size, it has three heat settings, and the stirrer can be disengaged.

Sperry's Black-Eyed Peas

(Serves 4)

Sperry's Restaurant in Nashville, at (615) 353-0809, has been a favorite dining spot and gathering place for locals and visitors alike since its opening in 1975. Judy Thomas, wife of co-owner Dick Thomas, cooked a big batch of black-eyed peas to serve at midnight on the eatery's first New Year's Eve. This was done in keeping with the Southern tradition of eating black-eyed peas on New Year's Day for good luck in the coming year. Since that time, black-eyed peas have become a Sperry's annual tradition. If you like, add a penny to the pot while cooking. Although I believe that the penny gives luck to all who eat the peas on New Year's Day, others believe that the person who gets the portion with the penny will get the luck—unless he or she swallows the penny—so be careful, and enjoy!

EQUIPMENT NEEDED: Slow cooker, food processor (or chopper)
PREPARATION TIME: 2–6 hours, depending on cooking temperature

INGREDIENTS
- **2 cups dried black-eyed peas, soaked overnight in cold water**
- **3–5 ounces smoked hog jowl (if not available, use equivalent amount of good-quality bacon)**
- **2 cups water**
- **½ medium-large onion**
- **½ tsp. Tabasco sauce**
- **1¼ tsp. salt**
- **2 tbs. flour**
- **freshly ground black pepper**

PREPARATION
- Drain the peas and put into slow cooker. Add meat.
- Add 2 cups water, onion (chopped in food processor), Tabasco, and salt.
- Cook until peas are tender (about 2½ to 3½ hours on High, or 5½ to 6 hours on Low).
- Remove meat.

- Whisk some flour into a small amount of water to create a smooth paste, and add to peas in Crock-Pot, stirring until thoroughly mixed.
- Cook for 30 minutes on Low.
- Season to taste with ground pepper.

Peanut Butter Machine: Salton's Just Nutty

$40

Peanut butter lovers will go nuts over this electronic unit that makes pure peanut butter with no added fats, oils, or emulsifiers. And, best of all, it is easy to use. Shaped like an oversized coffee-bean grinder, the Just Nutty features a 6-ounce nut holder, a grinding blade, and a 12-ounce removable container.

To use, just fill the nut holder and turn it on. Within seconds the nuts are ground into peanut butter, which is automatically dispensed into the removable container. The grind can be adjusted from chunky to smooth, and the unit pops apart for easy cleaning.

For the more adventurous, it can be used with almonds, cashews, or pistachios (shelled, of course). You can even grind sesame seeds to make tahini paste. Other than the obvious fun factor, the Just Nutty is ideal for making healthier peanut butter. Those on restricted diets may opt for dry-roasted or salt-free nuts. But whatever ingredients you choose, the finished product is as fresh as it gets, and it tastes great!

Best Multi-Use Waffle Iron: VillaWare's Belgian Waffle & Multi Baker

$90

Okay, so you can pick up a standard waffle iron at just about any
department store or gourmet
shop, but just exactly how often
are you going to make waffles anyway? And where are you going to
store it? There's already a slow cooker and deep fryer under the sink.
Besides, depending on where you live, a Waffle House, an IHOP, or
a Denny's is probably just around the corner.

VillaWare's unit solves the single-use dilemma with its multiple
personalities. First, it makes the thickest Belgian waffles in the business (4½ inches square by 1¼ inches deep). Remove its waffle plate
and insert its included flat griddle for pancakes, French toast, or
sandwiches. But that's not all! The unit also has a raised rib grill
attachment that converts it into an indoor grill, complete with ribs
that channel excess fats away. It features a stylish chrome exterior
and is relatively easy to clean.

Sandwich Sidekick: T-Fal's Sandwich Maker

$35

Although sandwich makers have been around almost as long as the
coffeemaker, it took the
infomercials of the 1980s to
make them a household necessity. Because of their compact
size and quick operation, sandwich makers are useful kitchen
appliances. They make great
sandwiches too. This unit fea-

tures enough room for two sandwiches, a preset thermostat, and an indicator light that tells you when it's time to cook. These devices are great with homes with kids, as you can make hot sandwiches in a jiffy.

This machine's top panel folds in a clamshell-like fashion over your creation, seals it inside, and automatically cuts each sandwich into triangular halves as well.

ICE-CREAM MAKERS

Forget the backbreaking, hand-cranking, messy ice-cream makers of yesteryear; the latest electronic ice-cream machines make preparing your favorite frozen treats easier than ever before.

Most electric machines use a disc that you freeze, then place in an insulated bowl with your ingredients. This eliminates the salt and ice required with the more traditional units. Best of all the machines have motors, which rotate the ingredients to create the ice cream— no cranking required.

Best Electric Ice-Cream Machine: Krups La Glaciere

$60

In only 30 minutes this miracle of modern technology creates up to 1½ quarts of ice cream, yogurt, or sorbet—that's almost faster than driving to/from the ice-cream store.

To prepare, just freeze its double-insulated work bowl overnight, then place it in the countertop machine. Put in your ingredients, and turn it on. It's that easy. Other features include a see-through plastic lid with feeder cap for adding chocolate chips or other goodies without interruption during churning, and a nice storage bowl container.

TWO HOT TRENDS IN COUNTERTOP APPLIANCES: INDOOR GRILLING AND INFUSION COOKING

Indoor Grilling

Disproving the old adage "Where there's smoke there's fire," the latest trend in the kitchen, indoor grilling, has neither smoke nor fire. A great way to BBQ year-round, indoor grills use science to their benefit and eliminate the smoke of outdoor grilling because the fats and juices of the meat drip into a prefilled water reservoir on the grill. When the hot juices hit the cool water, there is no smoke—what a concept! Another benefit to indoor grilling is that because the fat drips away into a reservoir, foods are healthier than when they cook in their own juices. The only negative to indoor grills is that they are space eaters and hard to store.

Best Indoor Grill: T-Fal Excelio Indoor BBQ & Griddle

$120

Everyone loves a good BBQ. But if the weather is not cooperating, or you just don't feel like fighting the bugs for your meal, then an indoor grill may be just the ticket.

Our pick for this year's best is the T-Fal Excelio grill. This 1,200-watt AC-powered unit features an adjustable thermostat, an 81-square-inch, nonstick cooking grate for meats, fish, and kabobs, and a griddle insert grate for flat-frying pancakes, bacon, veggies, and more.

Both grates are grooved and angled to channel fat and grease away from the food. Since the fat and grease never touch the heating elements, smoke is prevented from forming indoors. Because of its 10×16×3-inch size, it can be placed on the kitchen counter or directly on the dining room table when you entertain.

Stylish Indoor Grill: Hamilton Beach HealthSmart Indoor Grill

$75

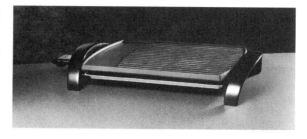

With Museum of Modern Art–type styling, this attractive 1,450-watt indoor grill looks good enough to keep on your countertop year-round.

It features a nonstick surface and two heat settings: a high heat for meats, and a medium heat for vegetables. Other features include nonskid feet, rounded grill bars that allow juices to drip away from food, and embedded heat elements that help provide more consistent grilling.

Fusion Cooking

According to our good friend and housewares trend-spotter Barb Westfield, fusion cooking is the next big thing in the kitchen.

Fusion cooking entails mixing herbs and lemons in water and cooking your meats, veggies, and the like on a lidded indoor grill over this scented infusion of herbs and spices.

Many restaurants are experimenting with this method, and soon there will be a number of products for the home that allow you to cook the same way. Like indoor grilling, fusion cooking also separates the fats from the meats, making it a healthy way to cook your foods as well.

Coolest Infusion Device: Salton's Volcano Infusion Grill

$100

Looking a bit like a volcano, this bizarre electric countertop indoor grill features a concave cooking area, a glass lid, and a round well to which you add a fusion of mixes for cooking meats, veggies, and more.

The water reservoir can be filled with anything from lemons to liquid smoke to herbs, and when you put its glass lid on, the aromatic steam blends with your food. Fats drip away as well for a healthier feast.

No word yet whether it erupts when you're finished.

CHAPTER 4

It's Party Time

Entertaining and Cleaning Products

$\mathbf{I}$f I were Martha Stewart, I would show you how to use a hot-glue gun to turn this book into a buffet-serving tray, recycle it with a bit of decoupage, and use it during your next party as a doily. But alas, I'm no Martha Stewart. Although I do like to entertain at home, unlike Martha, I do not enjoy spending tireless hours preparing the buffet and making candles from scratch; I would rather let the latest entertaining products help me do the work.

Whether you're feeding five or fifty, this chapter will help you find the right equipment to make your next event a smashing success—kind of like having the right tool for the right job. And because the biggest blowout often leads to the biggest messes, we've also tossed in a section with the latest and greatest cleaning products that will make the morning after easier than ever. So forget about converting last year's Christmas tree into beautiful buffet decorations, or recycling your brother-in-law's beer cans and using them to create a stunning aluminum fois gras serving dish, and let's do some living and entertaining the easy way—Gadget Guru–style.

SECTION I

Put Some Heat Under the Seat

Food Warmers

Whether you're setting up a buffet or a larger sit-down dinner, it is important to keep hot foods hot. After all, there is nothing worse than a cold broccoli-cheese casserole or congealed bowl of gravy—except, of course, your in-laws' reminding you that it's cold.

There are a variety of means to keep your foods piping hot. You can use electricity, canned heat like Sterno or butane, or some of the new cook-and-serve bakeware, or you can run to the microwave, as they do in restaurants when something is sent back because it's cold.

The best offense is a good defense, however; so before you entertain, it makes sense to purchase some products that promise to keep your food warm until the last guests make their way through the buffet. Here's a sample of some of our favorites:

Best Hors d'Oeuvres Food Warmer: Metrokane Hot Butler

$50

This is definitely the coolest "hot" product I've seen in a long time! Instead of using sterno, alcohol, or electricity to keep food warm, this unique buffet warmer uses two tiny tea candles as its heat source. It features a 16×12-inch superconductive aluminum top that absorbs the heat from the candles below and keeps the tray at an even 175 degrees F. for up to five hours.

To use, just place the unit on your table or buffet and light the two candles. About five minutes later, lower the hinged top so that it can begin absorbing the heat, and place your hors d'oeuvres directly on the lid or set a casserole or serving dish on top. The Hot Butler's base stays cool and can be safely placed on virtually any surface, including wood and tablecloths. Two tea candles are included.

Linda's Awesome Artichoke Dip

(Serves 10–12)

My sister, Linda Mossman, is a great cook—she has to be, as she has five little ones running around the house. But when she's invited out and needs to bring a covered dish, you can bet that it's her famous Artichoke Dip. Check it out; it's not only easy to prepare, it's a real crowd pleaser. Just serve with crackers or jumbo Fritos, place on the table, and watch it disappear.

EQUIPMENT NEEDED: food processor, baking dish
PREPARATION TIME: 30 minutes

INGREDIENTS
- **2 14-ounce cans artichoke hearts**
- **1½ cups grated Swiss cheese**
- **¾ cup grated Parmesan cheese**
- **1 cup mayonnaise**

PREPARATION
- Preheat oven to 350 degrees F.
- Drain artichokes and chop in food processor.
- Grate Swiss and Parmesan cheese in food processor.
- Mix all ingredients and stuff into a baking dish.
- Bake for 30 minutes.
- Serve with Fritos or crackers.

Best Big Buffet Server: West Bend Buffet Server

$210

For larger gatherings, you may want to take a look at West Bend's Buffet Server. This electric 22×10-inch stainless steel tray holds and warms three casserole dishes: one 3-quart, and two 1½-quart dishes. Each dish is removable for easy cleaning and has a lid that assists in keeping the food warm. An adjustable thermostat allows you to set the temperature between 165 degrees and 185 degrees F. It runs on AC power and easily converts into a warming tray.

Best Bread Warmer: Vesture Heated Bread Warmers

$30

You've baked a beautiful loaf of bread, but how do you keep it warm during your party or meal without burning it? These bread warmer baskets from Vesture will do the trick. These tabletop, basket-style bread warmers come complete with cloth napkin inserts and feature a heating pod that you place in the microwave for about three minutes, then reinsert in the pouch sewn into each napkin. Each pod will keep your bread warm for up to 3 hours at the table. The baskets come in three sizes: a French bread–length basket, an oval 1-pound for muffins and rolls, and an oval 2-pound for croissants or round loaves.

Best Buffet Cooktop: Mr. Max Portable Burner

$50

If you're cooking omelets, sautéing, or just need a good low-heat burner for your buffet, look no further than this portable unit from Burton. The square gas grill features three heat settings (Low, Medium, and High) and has a built-in ignition system—no matches required. Best of all, it's powered by butane canisters, which provide consistent, even heat on each setting. Other features include a drip pan to catch spills and overflows, and a cool-touch base for tabletop cooking.

This burner is versatile, as it is a great device to keep on hand to feed the family during the occasional power outage. You can take it camping or to your next tailgate party.

Fastest Way to the Buffet: Chantal's Cook and Serve Collection Grand Buffet and Buffet Casserole

$130 Grand Buffet, $100 Buffet Casserole

Eliminate clutter in your kitchen by buying pans like these that you can both cook and serve in. The Grand Buffet features an oval, 3-quart sauté-style casserole dish with handles, a stylish tempered-

glass lid, and a stainless steel stand with candleholder. It comes in a variety of cool colors too (blue, green, white, red).

The Buffet Casserole is a 3-quart-deep casserole dish with handles and a tempered-glass top, and comes with an elegant sculpted glass warming stand for prettying up the buffet. It comes in blue, green, white, red, light green, yellow, or light blue, so you'll have no trouble matching your décor.

Poochie's Mom's Easy Green Bean Casserole

(Serves 4–8)

Myrtle Kelley, aka Poochie's Mom, is John Kelley's grandmother. Poochie was her dog when John was a child. He took to calling her Poochie's Mom. Subsequently, all nine grandchildren, even the ones who never met Poochie, still lovingly refer to her as Poochie's Mom.

EQUIPMENT NEEDED: sauté-style casserole dish
PREPARATION TIME: 30 minutes

INGREDIENTS
- 1 14-ounce can green beans, or 1 pound fresh green beans if in season
- 1 14-ounce can green lima beans, or 1 pound fresh if you can get them
- 2 cans mushroom soup
- 1 can of french-fried onion crisps

PREPARATION
- Preheat oven to 350 degrees F.
- Drain the beans and pour into casserole dish.
- Add mushroom soup.
- Bake for 25 minutes, or until ingredients bubble.
- Sprinkle the onion crisps over the casserole and serve piping hot.

Microwave Food Warmer Plate: The Vesture Heatwave Microwavable Hotplate

$25

Instead of having to plug it in to get power, you just pop this 9½-inch square ceramic heating tile in the microwave for 4 minutes. It then keeps the food warm on the table or buffet for about an hour.

With enough room for a soup plate, gravy bowl, or plate of hors d'oeuvres, its Microcore center disperses heat evenly at 300 degrees F. for about 60 minutes. Its outer casing, which frames the tile, remains cool to the touch and protects the counter surface.

SECTION II

Fabulous Fondues

One of the great joys of cooking fondue-style is its communal effect—everyone at your party can get involved and have fun while doing the final preparations. Other than being the center of a social event, most fondues are relatively easy to set up and use—really! The only thing you need for a fondue party is a fondue set, Sterno (unless your set is electrically powered), some oil, cheese, and bread, and you're ready to go. Of course, fondues are not just for cheese. You can create thousands of delicious dips from lobster to chocolate, and there are as many things you can dip in the fondue.

For the past seven winters, the *Today* show has sent us to the mountains to report on the latest in ski equipment. In three of those seven years, we have found ourselves visiting Sugarbush, Vermont. Of course, after a rough day on the slopes we often head out to sample the local restaurants. Our favorite French restaurant in Sugarbush (actually it's the only French restaurant in Sugarbush) is called Henri's. It is owned and operated by our buddy, named—you guessed it—Henri. One of our favorite appetizers is Henri's cheese fondue. This dish, which he serves at the bar, sticks to your ribs and keeps you warm during those cold winter nights.

During ski season at Henri's, you can drop by and enjoy some fondue at the bar while waiting to eat. While you're there, make sure you attempt to climb the legendary bar pole in the center of the room. If you succeed (and only a few have—ski legend Jean-Claude Killy being one of them), you'll get your name on the ceiling and a free bottle of champagne too. Did I mention that you can't use your legs? That explains why, after all these years, Henri's still has a cooler full of champagne!

Famous Fondue Set: Burton's Revolving 15-Piece Fondue Set

$50

The best fondue set we've seen is the Burton 15-piece set. What separates this one from the pack is its unique lazy Susan–like rack that holds up to 6 cups of your favorite dipping materials around the pot. This arrangement allows you to have all your ingredients on the turntable for easy poking into the pot.

The 15-piece set includes a white-enamel-on-steel fondue pot with stainless steel top and wooden handle, 6 stainless steel 2-pronged dipping (fondue) forks with wooden handles, and 6 white ceramic condiment cups. Its stylish stainless steel base/stand has a removable metal Sterno cup with a matching cap to extinguish the flame.

Sweet Fondue Set: Chantal Chocolate Fondue

$40

Designed for dipping, this tiny cobalt-blue pot holds 2½ cups of your fondue dip. Perfect for dipping strawberries and cookies in chocolate or for dipping your favorite chips into, it also makes a great sauce-warmer for the buffet.

It comes with a stainless steel base that holds a standard tea candle and 2 dipping forks.

SECTION III

Seafood Sensations

If you're hooked on fish, crustaceans, and other famous treats from the deep blue sea, then you know that it takes certain types of tools to prepare them.

Of course you don't have to entertain to cook fish, but if you go to all the trouble to purchase a big lobster pot, boiling pan, poacher, or even an oyster shucker, why not throw a party? Maybe your guests will even help with the cleanup! Yeah, right!

Super Seafood Prep Tools:
OXO Seafood Tool Collection
$5–$12

Featuring OXO's famous ergonomic handles, these tools will make prepping your favorite crustaceans, well, almost fun. This lineup includes a clam knife, shrimp cleaner, oyster knife, and seafood cracker.

Mom's (Madeline Pargh's) Potato Soup

(Serves 6)

My mom is a wonderful cook. As I mentioned previously, she has the amazing talent of quickly throwing a complete meal together with ingredients she has on hand and making it taste like she was cooking all day. If my dad has one favorite recipe of Mom's, it has to be her potato soup. Mom has closely guarded this recipe, but now it's yours to enjoy. Please note that this recipe is nondairy—but your guests will never know.

EQUIPMENT NEEDED: large stockpot, sauté pan
PREPARATION TIME: about an hour

INGREDIENTS
- **6 medium potatoes, cut into cubes**
- **3 carrots, sliced**
- **3 stalks celery, sliced**
- **2 onions, chopped separately**
- **6 cups chicken stock**
- **2 tbs. margarine**
- **2 tbs. flour**
- **Salt and pepper to taste**
- **4 sprigs parsley, chopped**

PREPARATION
- Put potatoes, carrots, celery, one chopped onion, and the chicken stock in the stockpot and cook until tender.
- Sauté the other chopped onion in margarine until lightly brown.
- Mix in flour to thicken.
- Add one cup of liquid from stockpot to the sauté pan, and stir until smooth.
- Pour contents of sauté pan into soup.
- Stir and cook until thickened; add seasoning to taste and garnish with chopped parsley.

Best Stockpot Set: Metro Marketing's 8-, 12-, 16-, and 20-Quart Aluminum Stockpot Set

$60

Whether you're boiling up a batch of crawfish, a batch of shrimp, or a couple of lobsters, a big stockpot is the order of the day. This set of pots will help any cook prepare a big feast. Each piece features a lid and water-fill indentations on its outer body so you can see your fill line.

Great for fresh ears of corn, boiling lots of pasta, or Mrs. Pargh's Potato Soup (see page 120), this pot will definitely get the job done.

SECTION IV

Casual Entertaining

Picking Perfect Products for a Patch of Couch Potatoes

Whether it's having the buddies over for the Super Bowl, a weekly poker fest, or just watching a movie at home on the big screen TV, casual entertaining is one of the most popular ways to get together with your friends.

For many, this type of entertaining means merely pouring a bag of Doritos in a bowl and popping open a can of dip. But even the most informal of parties can include some delicious and easy-to-make foods that you can prepare in minutes. The good news is that if you take just the few minutes it takes to prepare it yourself, you'll find that it costs about half of what you'd spend at the local 7-11 or from ordering a few pizzas from the Domino's down the street. And since Domino's no longer guarantees delivery in 30 minutes or less, you can probably do it quicker, too.

This section will give you a look at products and show you some easy recipes that promise to delight even the most hard-boiled couch potatoes. From popcorn makers to dip-and-chip bowls to perfect pizza cutters and other specialty snack stuff, go ahead and put your feet up on the table, because we're here to serve.

POPCORN POPPERS

Every year Americans consume over a billion pounds of popcorn. Who told us that? The Popcorn Institute, of course! The Chicago Popcorn Institute, to be exact, a hallowed place where great minds gather to pop corn and contemplate kernels. (And you thought *we* had a cushy job!)

While there's nothing more convenient than tossing a bag of popcorn into the microwave, there are other methods that are almost as easy and that deliver kernels that, depending on the method of preparation, can be healthier. One of our favorite popcorn-making gadgets is a hand-cranked, stovetop popcorn maker.

**Best Hand-Cranked
Popcorn Popper:
The Whirley Pop**

$35

If you like really good popcorn, bypass the microwave and try out this nifty gadget. This aluminum 6-quart stovetop popper features an elongated wooden stirring paddle that makes delicious hand-cranked popcorn in just 3 minutes. To use, just add your ingredients to the popper, place it on the stovetop, and start cranking. This action rotates a paddle inside the pan, evenly coating the kernels with oil and keeping them moving so they don't burn. The cranking paddle ensures that every single kernel pops up to 42 times its original size, while its built-in steam vents eliminate any chance of soggy popcorn. Try that with the microwave stuff!

In addition to fluffier and dryer popcorn, the Whirley Pop takes the corn to 475 degrees F., allowing you to add flavored seasonings like special chocolate, butterscotch, caramel, or Southwestern flavor right into the pan, where the kernels absorb all the spices.

Its paddle crank makes healthier popcorn as well, because it requires less oil than even the light popcorn brands found on super-market shelves. The Whirley Pop includes three mixes, a popper, and a recipe booklet.

Best Party Tray: Holdems Handles All

$20 for 6

You've seen the commercial—a group of folks are going through the buffet, and because the host has provided flimsy paper plates, the guests are fumbling around trying to keep from spilling the fare all over the brand-spanking-new white carpet. Forget the Styrofoam; here's something better—in fact it's so sturdy, there's a better-than-average chance that John "Crash" Kelley could make it through the buffet line without a single spill!

The Holdems Handles All are 12×11-inch plastic trays that hold just about everything your guests can possibly carry away from the buffet.

Made of dishwasher-safe plastic, these trays feature 3 beverage holder indentations: one for a 12-ounce can, a unique stem clip for a wine/champagne glass, and a third for a cup. But that's not all; they also feature a plate indentation and 2 pockets for utensils and napkins.

To hold, simply place your fingers through both utensil holes or put your thumb through the wineglass hole. They're great for picnics, buffets, or just dinner on the couch.

Aunt Maria's (Maria Pargh's) Party-Sized Potato Salad

(Serves 20)

My brother is the luckiest guy in the world. If you ever had the opportunity to meet his wife, Maria, you'd agree. Aside from her numerous other attributes, she is definitely one of the best cooks around. In fact, I should forget about putting together recipes and pass this responsibility on to her. This potato salad recipe is absolutely the best you will ever have. Even better, it's easy to duplicate. Give it a try; it goes great with fried chicken, hamburgers, hot dogs, turkey sandwiches, corned beef sandwiches, soup, steak, lamb chops. . . . Hey, stop me before I start sounding like Forrest Gump's friend Bubba!

EQUIPMENT NEEDED: food processor, mixing bowl, large stockpot
PREPARATION TIME: 30 minutes

INGREDIENTS
- 1 14-ounce can jumbo pitted black olives
- 1½ cups celery
- 1 medium onion
- 2 medium green peppers
- ½ cup pimentos
- 10 pounds russet potatoes
- 1 cup parsley
- 32 ounces Miracle Whip
- 3 tbs. mustard
- Salt and pepper to taste

PREPARATION
- Chop olives, celery, onion, peppers, and pimento in a food processor or by hand.
- Wash potatoes and boil with skin on until tender (a knife can slide easily in and out). Let them cool; peel and cut into quarters.
- In a large mixing bowl combine potatoes, chopped vegetables, and parsley. Stir in Miracle Whip and mustard. Salt and pepper to taste and garnish with chopped parsley.
- Chill and serve on the Fourth of July—or anytime!

Snack Bowl from Hell: Oinking Snackbowl

$25

Forget Fen-Phen or all those other dietary supplements; this Oinking Snackbowl will keep you and everyone else out of the snacks. An invisible radio frequency field located about 4 inches above the bowl ensures that every time a hand crosses the zone, an obnoxious Oinking sound will automatically belly out of the swine-shaped bowl, making it impossible to sneak a snack when nobody is looking. It's powered by 4 AA batteries and is sure to be a hit at your next get-together.

No word yet if they have made a George Castanza model that signals to the guests when someone double-dips, a move perfected on *Seinfeld*.

A Duplex for Chips and Dip: Ullman's Pool Chip n Dip

$4

Whether you're poolside or lounging on the couch, this colorful aquatic-themed serving plate delivers your dip and chips in perfect order.

It features two wells inside the plate: a larger kidney swimming pool–shaped chip holder that holds a big bag of chips, and a smaller kiddy pool–shaped dip holder that holds 8 ounces of dip.

Constructed of unbreakable hard plastic, it can be used indoors or out and is dishwasher safe. Also available is a matching collection of pitchers, highball glasses, and tumblers.

PIZZA: THE PERFECT PARTY FOOD

Don't Call Domino's: Wolfgang Puck's Pizza at Home Kit

$50

If pizza is your fare of choice, instead of ordering out you may want to consider making it yourself. This hot Pizza at Home kit from famed chef Wolfgang Puck, owner of Spagos restaurants, could be just the ticket for making the perfect pizza.

It features everything you need—except the pizza, of course—to bake a perfect pie every time. Included with the 15-inch lipped ceramic-covered pizza stone are a serving rack, a pizza cutter, and a serving spatula.

Of course, the package wouldn't be complete without a selection of Puck's famous recipes.

Howard Kirshner's Killer Clam Dip

(Serves 4)

I've known Howard Kirshner almost all of my life. (I would say all of my life, but Howard is a few years my junior.) Howard has always had a flair for cooking—and eating what he has prepared. Years ago, when we both lived in Knoxville, I would occasionally drop over Howard's apartment for burgers. Yes, they were great, but Howard had one vice—an addiction to Heinz Ketchup. He would put it on everything except his clam dip. Howard and his lovely wife, Leslie, have many friends, and get invited to numerous get-togethers. The invitations often come with one request: BRING A BIG BOWL OF CLAM DIP. Oh, and one other thing: Howard, whatcha doing for the Super Bowl? Can you bring some dip?

EQUIPMENT NEEDED: mixing bowl, hand mixer
PREPARATION TIME: 10 minutes

INGREDIENTS
- 1 6½-ounce can of Doxee minced clams, drained
- ¼ cup clam juice from drained clams
- 1 tsp. Minute Maid lemon juice concentrate
- ¾ tsp. Worcestershire sauce
- ½ tsp. onion salt
- ½ tsp. garlic powder
- 1 8-ounce brick Philadelphia low-fat cream cheese

PREPARATION
- Drain clams, reserving ¼ cup of the juice.
- In a mixing bowl, mix clams, clam juice, lemon juice, Worcestershire sauce, onion salt, and garlic powder.
- Add cheese and use hand mixer to blend.
- Let chill overnight (if you can keep your hands out of it).
- Serve with chips, pepper crackers, or veggies.

Best Pizza Oven: Gino's East Deep Dish Pizza Kit

$100

If you've always wanted to be able to prepare true Chicago-style deep-dish pizza at home but without the mess, this unit is for you! Licensed and tested by its namesake, the world-famous Chicago-based pizza restaurant chain, this standalone deep-dish pizza oven is the perfect product for preparing your favorite pies.

The kit includes a round electric 12×1½-inch-deep nonstick aluminum cooking surface with an embedded heating element and a lid. All you do is prepare the dough, add the ingredients, and close the lid. Because of its tight-sealing lid, a loaded deep-dish pizza is ready in 20 minutes.

But best of all, Gino's supplies pizza ingredients (five-pack: $25), including special prepackaged flour mixes, from its restaurant for authentic New York, Chicago, and whole wheat pizzas, as well as recipes that provide super pies for the Super Bowl.

Because it heats evenly, with no hot spots, it is also ideal for preparing thin-crusted pizzas or for heating frozen pizzas.

Craziest Pizza Cutter: Rock n Roll Pizza Cutter

$2

Instead of a unicycle, this pizza cutter looks like a mini seesaw. It has no sharp blade, yet it cuts a 12-inch pizza in one simple rocking motion. Amazing, huh?

To cut your pie, cheeses, or even sandwiches, just grasp its handle and gently rock the cutter back and forth. The pressure cuts a perfect slice every time, and it's both kid and dishwasher safe.

FIESTA TIME

Tacos, tortillas, quesadillas, nachos, and salsa not only make excellent dinner items but are great party foods as well, because they are easy to prepare. Since most items can be eaten with your fingers, they don't require any silverware, making for an easy cleanup session after the party.

Terrific Taco Plate: Taco Time Taco Plate

$2.50

Everybody loves tacos, but the reason you don't see them at many parties is that they are difficult to serve. Once the guests have gone through the line and loaded up the crispy shells with ground beef, tomatoes, cheese, and the like, there's just no easy way to keep the ingredients from spilling out of the taco before you take the first bite.

To the rescue comes the Taco Time Taco Plate. Featuring deep wells that hold 2 tacos upright without spilling over and enough room for 2 side dishes as well, this plate will be the hit of your next taco party. Best of all, they sell for just $2.50 each, so you can order plenty and give one to each guest. The best news is that because of its design, there will be less mess to clean off the floor.

Unfortunately, there's still no easy way to bite into the taco.

Linda's Mexican Tortilla Casserole

(Serves 4)

My sister Linda loves to entertain. But when you stop and think about it, with 5 little ones (ages 5 to 15) and a husband (much older), just dinner for 7 is a feat in itself. So, when she has friends over, whether it's casual or formal, Linda is right at home organizing any event. After her guests have munched on her famous artichoke dip (see page 113), they can head to the buffet and pick up a slice of her Mexican Tortilla Casserole.

EQUIPMENT NEEDED: food processor, 8-inch glass pie dish
PREPARATION TIME: 20 minutes

INGREDIENTS
- 1 14½-ounce can Mexican-style stewed tomatoes
- ⅓ cup packed chopped fresh cilantro
- 5 6-inch corn tortillas
- 1½ cups shredded Monterey Jack cheese
- sour cream
- sliced black olives
- shredded lettuce

PREPARATION
- Preheat oven to 450 degrees F.
- Puree tomatoes and ¼ cup cilantro in food processor or chopper.
- Spread ¼ of puree in bottom of pie dish.
- Top with 1 tortilla.
- Sprinkle ⅓ cup of cheese on top.
- Repeat layering in this order: tortilla, ⅓ cup cheese, ¼ cup sauce.
- Top with last tortilla sauce and cheese.
- Bake until sauce bubbles (about 10 minutes).
- Remove, and sprinkle remaining cilantro.
- Garnish with cold sour cream, black olives, and shredded lettuce.
- Cut into wedges and serve with Pacifica, a delicious Mexican beer.

Mexican Restaurant in a Box: Salton/Maxim Taco Bell Kitchen Original Line

Quesadilla Oven $35

Enchilada/Omelet Grill $25

Mini Food Processor $40

Make a run for the border with Salton's new Taco Bell Kitchen Originals line, which includes a chrome-plated Tortilla and Quesadilla Oven, an Enchilada and Mexican Omelet Oven/Grill, and a Mini Food Processor/Chopper.

The Tortilla/Quesadilla Oven is similar to a waffle iron in size. It opens in a clamshell-like fashion and has heating elements on both the top and bottom plates for cooking tortillas and quesadillas on the spot. To make a quesadilla, just place a tortilla in the unit, put your ingredients on top, place another tortilla on top of your ingredients, and close the oven. It does the rest in less than one minute. It's also great for warming tortillas for burritos.

The Enchilada and Mexican Omelet Oven is square-shaped and looks amazingly similar to the sandwich makers of yesteryear. It too opens in a clamshell-like fashion, allowing you to load your ingredients and cook them on both heating elements much faster than a conventional oven. In fact, this unit can evenly cook burritos in about 5 to 10 minutes, compared to 40 minutes in a regular oven. You can also make sandwiches or use the cooktop as a grill to warm vegetables for fajitas or quesadillas. Oh, did I mention that when opened, it makes a great omelet pan too?

The Mini Food Processor/Chopper allows you to whip up a quick batch of guacamole, salsa, or a spicy dip in no time. It features a stainless steel chopping blade and 2 bowls, including one that automatically releases chopped food through a handy chute.

SECTION V

Beverage Bonanza

Quintessential Products for the Thirsty Guest

Now that you're prepared to feed the mob, you've got to give them something to drink too. This section features a cornucopia of cool devices to help you serve your beverages at your next event.

Grooviest Party Drink Maker:
Black & Decker's Partymate Drinkmaker

$70

One of the best ideas to hit blenders since Jimmy Buffet made margaritas a household name is Black & Decker's cordless blender. This 32-ounce blender can go anywhere— yes, I mean anywhere. That's because it operates on Black & Decker's Versa Pack Batteries. This is the first product that not only can make a frozen screwdriver but can power one too! That's because the same batteries that power numerous Black & Decker power tools also power this blender. So you can make a screwdriver, or power one, with the same battery. Productive, huh?

But don't let its cordless makeup fool you; it still has plenty of power. Enough to crush ice and make daiquiris for the whole pool, campsite, and tailgate party, or just enough to use out on the back deck or while you relax on a boat. Each charge lasts for approximately 3 gallons of crushed ice mixes. Other features include a stainless steel blade and a 32-ounce Plexiglas pitcher.

WINE NOT: RANDY RAYBURN'S TOP 10 WINE TIPS

Restaurateur and sommelier Randy Rayburn is a good friend and even better host. Stop by one of his Nashville restaurants—The Sunset Grill, (615) 386-3663, or Midtown Café. Both offer one of the largest by-the-glass selections of wine in the Southeast. Great food, too.

1. Get a wine opener (see below); take your time opening.
2. Ask questions of your server or salesperson.
3. Red wine CAN go with fish (for example, Pinot Noir with salmon).
4. Simple foods call for complex wine.
5. Complex food calls for simple wine.
6. Do not overchill white wines.
7. Lightly chill Pinots/Burgundies (room temperature is not the same around the world).
8. Pour wine only a third of the way up the glass (gives it room to breathe).
9. Buy wine by the case—it's cheaper!
10. Don't sniff the cork—IT SMELLS LIKE A CORK!

Best Wine Cooler: Metrokane's Cooler Cooler

$15

This product is so cool they named it twice. This stylish wine sleeve or cooler keeps your vino at the temperature you've chilled it to for 2 hours after opening. Best of all, there's

no need to add ice or water because its thermal insulated carafe holds in the temperature.

Unlike other wine coolers, the Cooler Cooler does not generate condensation, so you can safely put it on the tabletop or buffet.

Best Value Wine Opener: OXO Wine Opener

$20

This ergonomically designed wine opener makes it easy to uncork your wine with its oversized knoblike handle. Great for left-handers too, as you can turn it in either direction to remove the cork.

It also features a built-in label cutter for removing labels or price tags.

Ultimate Wine Opener: The Screwpull

$140

If you serve lots of wine, or just could never get the hang of those inexpensive openers, this is the wine opener for you. Looking like a reduced-in-size version of those professional wine openers found mounted on the bar at your favorite restaurant, this handy device uses a process called mechanical leverage to remove even the toughest cork from a wine bottle. To use, just place the corkscrew over the cork and press the handle downward, and the cork magically pops out—no straining, turning, or twisting required. You don't even have to twist the cork off the screw. Just pull the lever down and it ejects.

Other features include a C-shaped label cutter that makes a perfect incision around wine seals. Also included are one spare corkscrew blade and a handsome black storage box.

Most Bizarre Wine Product: The Vintage Enhancer

$70

It goes without saying that we deal with just about every manufacturer and public relations person on the planet. These folks get paid to pitch us products. While some of them constantly drive us crazy, there are a few that we really enjoy dealing with, one of whom is Greg Bond.

Greg is an importer of unique devices, and he travels the globe looking for new gadgets that promise to make life simpler and more fun. Okay, he's probably in it for the money, but every time he calls us about his latest find, he keeps us in stitches while he's telling us how it will save the planet. While we may pass on some of them, others we can't resist, as they sound too good to be true. The Vintage Enhancer falls into this latter category.

For those who enjoy wine with their meals, the Vintage Enhancer is a product that improves the taste of even the most inexpensive brands. This product makes the cheap stuff taste like the good stuff.

After consulting with a few wine connoisseurs, I learned that it's the delicate balance of the fruity flavor and tannic acids that creates the flavor of a specific wine. The Vintage Enhancer, which looks like a wine cooler, uses an electronic method to reduce the bitter taste found in some lower-priced wines. To use, just place an opened (but recorked) bottle of wine in the bucket, and plug it in. The Enhancer emits low-amp magnetic waves that pass through the bottle, effectively reducing the wine's tannic acids and consequently bitter taste. Sounds like a science experiment, doesn't it?

Since neither John nor myself are considered to be wine experts, we tried a different experiment to put this product through its paces. We purchased two identical bottles of grapefruit juice and placed one in the unit for about 20 minutes. The results were amazing. The bottle that had been placed in the Vintage Enhancer was much smoother and less bitter-tasting than the one that was not. My wine-loving friends had the same results when they conducted the test on wine.

Bond states that with red wines, the Vintage Enhancer breaks down the acid much as aging does over time. The Enhancer doesn't actually age the wine, but it can take a highly tannic libation and make it taste 5 years older in just 30 minutes.

He is also quick to note that other alcoholic beverages, such as Scotch whisky, bourbon, and cognac, also contain acids. The Vintage Enhancer can tame the strong bite of a 5-year-old bottle of scotch, making it as mellow as a 20-year-old aged bottle.

Is this product too good to be true? Well, being a country boy, I am not considered to be a wine connoisseur, but my experience with grapefruit juice tells me this product could very well be considered revolutionary.

We can't wait to see Greg's next trick!

Electric Wine Opener: Cava Stappi (That's Italian for "Wine Screw")

$100

The waiting's over; here's his next trick:

Automate, automate, and automate. Words to live by in any industry, but especially in housewares.

Yes, it's Napa Valley meets Silicon Valley with this new electric

wine opener. To open your vino, just remove the protective foil from the bottle, slide the Cava Stappi over the bottle's neck, and press the Power button. This action causes the corkscrew to rotate into the cork. A few seconds later the cork is removed. Press the Reverse button and it delivers the cork back to you in perfect shape. The whole process takes about 5 seconds. This product will definitely turn heads when you open your next bottle.

The Cava Stappi is powered by a rechargeable battery and includes an AC charging adapter.

Best-Dressed Wine Product: The Wine Butler

$5

Now that you've made the cheap stuff taste like the good stuff, you can afford to get a nice outfit for the bottle. Enter the Wine Butler, a line of clothing for—you guessed it—wine bottles.

Forget Barbie's and Ken's clothes; this apparel dresses up your vino in style. Available with miniature bow ties and vests or in more festive Fourth of July–themed clothing or New Year's tuxes, these fashionable duds come complete with buttons and an apronlike tie in the back. Slip one over the bottle's neck so it won't feel so naked at your next function. Okay, so I'm stretching it a bit. Here at the Gadget Guru we see everything—I mean everything—even clothing for wine bottles. Consider this to dress up your next dinner party.

CHAMPAGNE POPPING TIPS

Mention the millennium to champagne and sparkling-wine makers and you'll see dollar signs flash in their eyes. It's not long before the biggest party ever erupts on the planet, so it's a good idea to practice your cork-popping techniques—that is, unless you want to repair holes left in the ceiling by flying corks. Here are some handy safety tips on opening bubbly from *The Old Farmer's Almanac*.

- Keep the bottle cold. A warm bottle is more likely to pop unexpectedly. Champagne tastes best at 45 degrees F.
- Peel off the foil, and then carefully remove the wire hood while holding the cork down with the palm of your hand.
- Point the bottle away from yourself and others. Place a towel over the entire top and tilt the bottle at a 45 degree angle. Grasp the cork, slowly and firmly twisting it to break the seal.
- Keeping the bottle at a 45 degree angle, hold it firmly with one hand, using the other to slowly turn the cork with a slight upward pull. Do this until the cork is almost out of the neck. Counter the force of the cork by using slight downward pressure just as the cork breaks free of the bottle.
- For a stubborn cork, place the bottle under cool running tap water for about 20 seconds, and repeat the slow twisting under the towel.

TWO HOT, HOT DRINK PARTY PRODUCTS

Cordless Teakettle: Chef's Choice Cordless Electric Tea Kettle

$120

This terrific portable tea maker features a 1,500-watt electric base pad that boils the water in the kettle at the buffet or on a countertop. Once the water is boiled, the stylish kettle can be removed for easy serving of hot water for tea or soups.

Made of 18/10-grade stainless steel (see chapter 2 for explanation), the kettle holds 1⅓ quarts of water and has a cool touch base for setting on countertops or serving stations. Other features include an automatic shutoff when the water boils, and a safety shutoff valve on the pad as well.

Best Coffee/Espresso/ Cappuccino Maker for Entertaining: Capresso C2000

$1,395

This Rolls Royce of espresso machines not only makes the perfect latte and cappuccino on the market, it's fully automatic, grinding the beans, tamping, and brewing your espresso, all with the touch of a button.

Featuring an 18-bar power pump (a good thing), this unit allows you to make a single cup of espresso, 2 cups at the same time, a 16-ounce cup of cappuccino, or 2 mugs of coffee. It even has a hot water button for hot tea. It's fully automatic—meaning all you have to do is insert the beans in its 10-ounce bean container.

This is great for entertaining; its 96-ounce water reservoir can make 60 espressos or 19 cups of coffee continuously. Other features include a constant steam release for cappuccino, a 96-ounce removable water container, a separate funnel for preground coffee, and an automatic hot water cleaning and descaling program that keeps your machine spick and span. Measuring 14×15×13¾ inches, the C2000 fits easily underneath your kitchen cabinets.

SECTION VI

How to Cure the Postparty Cleaning Blues

Best Tile-Cleaning Device: Black & Decker Scum Buster

$60

Let's face it; when it comes to chores you love to hate, cleaning the tile in your kitchen (or your bathroom) has to be one of the most dreaded jobs of all. Tackling this headache head-on is the Black & Decker Scum Buster, a unique motorized scrubbing device that makes cleaning, well, almost fun. Powered by Black & Decker's popular Versa Pack rechargeable battery system (the same batteries that power the cordless Drinkmaker; see page 132), this cordless handheld scrubber comes with three attachable tools: a 4-inch scouring pad for the tub and tile, a 2-inch round detail brush for getting rid of dirt nestled around fixtures and corners, and a short-bristled 4-inch brush for cleaning the grout lines between your tiles.

Encased in a plastic coating, the Scum Buster motor unit is waterproof and weighs only 1¼ pounds. It has an ergonomic handle for an easy grip and a trigger-mounted button (like a drill) for easy operation. Each battery provides 25 minutes of run time (2 batteries and the charger are included) and best of all, the batteries can be used in other Black & Decker Versa Pack tools and household products.

Best Multipurpose Cleaner: Bissell Little Green Plus

$110

Spot cleaners can be valuable around-the-house tools—especially if you have a John Kelley lurking in the house (or office). John is a spiller; you can tell where he's been by following the trail of coffee on the carpet. That's why his wife prohibits him from drinking coffee in carpeted rooms. He is also a bit clumsy; that's why he's often called Crash. In fact, in his previous life as a bartender, he broke so many glasses that the bar lost money when he was in charge. John was the perfect person to test Bissell's Little Green Plus.

This is a product that helps keep him out of trouble, because when a spill occurs, this unit provides a fast, easy method of preserving carpets and floors. My favorite spot cleaners are not the big bulky units that take up valuable storage space, they are the little ones that set up quickly and are easy to maneuver. This year's best is Bissell's Little Green Plus.

What separates this unit from the pack is that it not only shampoos and cleans up spots and spills, it does windows too! Built in to the unit are a 5-foot 6-inch flexible hose, 2 removable tanks (one for a mixture of cleaning solution and hot water, one for the discharge), and a 20-foot power cord. Its on-board carpet/upholstery cleaning tool attachment consists of a 4-inch-wide scrub brush that connects to the hose. When you press its trigger, you release a high-pressure spray that breaks down the stain and draws it into the discharge tank. Its glass cleaning attachment has a trigger and a squeegee with suction that allows you to spray a solution of glass cleaner and hot tap water on your window/linoleum floor or mirror and suction it off. This eliminates the need for rags or paper towels and leaves a streak-free surface. Spring cleaning was never so easy.

➤Tip: Instead of using store-bought cleaners and paper towels to clean your windows and other glass, try vinegar with wadded-up old newspapers. It really makes your glass streak-free and shiny!

Best Electronic Mop: Dirt Devil Mop/Vac

$100

This innovative floor care device makes cleaning the kitchen floor easier than ever. It does this by combining sponge mopping and vacuuming in one unit—no hauling around messy buckets of water.

The cordless, rechargeable Mop Vac speeds drying time on linoleum, tile, and hardwood floors. First it dispenses the cleaning solution; then a sponge mop lifts the dirt and a vacuum draws the dirt into a holding tank. The unit weighs a mere 5 pounds and can clean up to 450 square feet on a 12-hour charge.

Ultimate Kitchen Trash Can: The MagicKan

$45

This trash can makes taking out the garbage—well, almost fun. Instead of loading individual garbage bags, the MagicKan conceals a 76-foot long continuous bag liner that connects to the lid of its 12-gallon can. A door in the front has a safety cutter mounted on the inside. Users simply fill the bag as

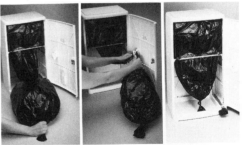

much or little as needed, then cut the end and either knot or twist tie. There's even a storage area for the twist ties. Tie another knot in the bag left behind, and the can is lined and ready to be filled again. Sound confusing? It's really not. In fact, with this unit you'll never touch your trash again.

CHAPTER 5

Big-Ticket Items

Ranges, Cooktops, Refrigerators, and Dishwashers

The kitchen ain't what it used to be. In the old days, the kitchen was the room set aside for the sole purpose of preparing meals. In fact, older kitchens barely have enough room for more than one family member to be able to walk around without bumping into each other. This has changed.

Today's kitchens are the center of social activity not only with room to prepare and cook meals, but with areas for friends and family members to gather and talk about the day's events. Many newly constructed homes are reflecting this trend, offering larger kitchen areas with more room to sit, socialize, or even watch TV. Recently, when I was shopping for a new home, I witnessed this trend first-hand. Many of the newer homes I viewed had kitchen/den or kitchen/living room combinations that made it difficult to see where the kitchen ended and the other room began. This was accomplished with the use of "islands," often including barstools that invited others to join in the conversation while the meal was being prepared. This new focus on the kitchen has also sparked a technology boom, resulting in more stylish and efficient big-ticket kitchen appliances like ranges, cooktops, refrigerators, and dishwashers. But don't let the phrase "big ticket" scare you, as appliances come in all price ranges.

Kitchen appliances are known in the industry as durables because, unlike a typical coffeemaker that will require replacement every few years, ranges, cooktops, refrigerators, and dishwashers are built to last for years on end. If you haven't shopped for one of these appliances lately, boy, are you in for a surprise. Many of these offerings are as high tech as any PC on the market—but they last longer and they help feed you too! Something Bill Gates can't do—yet, but I have a feeling he's working on it!

This chapter will examine the pros and cons of the different types of ranges and cooktops on the market, from gas and electric to a new space age technology called induction. We'll preview the hottest new cooktops and ovens on the market, look inside the refrigerator and the dishwasher, and show you some new concepts in water purification too. Don't need one of these big-ticket items? Don't worry—compendium B features handy tips and easy appliance repairs designed to keep your existing units going and going and going.

SECTION I

Cooktop Shop

Unless you enjoy the caveman lifestyle and are still cooking over an open fire, there are essentially two different fuels used for cooking food on a cooktop or in an oven: electricity and gas. However, there are a number of ways to use each of these energy sources to cook your foods. This section will inform you of the variety of choices available in cooktops and ovens.

AN EYE FOR AN EYE: BURNER FACTS, A BUYING GUIDE

Gas Burners (Conventional Gas Burner)

What is it? Heat comes from blue flame produced by burning the proper mixture of gas and air.

Pros: Immediate on/off control. A wide range of temperatures. Easy to operate. Efficient; minimal heat is retained after burner is turned off. Most flexible for different pan types and sizes.

Cons: Flame can go out on very low settings, and even the lowest simmer setting can be too hot for certain foods. Alas, cleanup is more time-consuming with gas than with electric.

Buying tip: Make sure it includes electronic ignition and sturdy grates that support all types of pots and pans.

Sealed Gas Burner

What is it? Operates like a conventional gas burner, but burners are sealed to the cooktop, preventing spills from flowing into hard-to-reach spots.

Pros: More stylish, easy to clean, maintains low heat (simmer) setting well. Generally performs like conventional gas units, but simmering is improved because flame is more spread out.

Cons: Porcelainized lighter-colored grates may require more frequent cleaning.

Buying tip: Look for grates that are easy to remove for cleaning and that stay stable with different sizes of pots and pans. Make sure that the burners include a simmer setting.

Electric Elements/Electric Coil

What is it? Electric resistance wiring encased in an insulated tube transfers heat from hot coil to cookware.

Pros: Heats up relatively quickly and has infinite heat settings. The coils are self-cleaning, as most spills will burn off.

Cons: Coils retain heat longer than gas after they're turned off—so keep the little ones away. Older pans with warped bottoms may not sit well on electric coils.

Buying tip: Look for coils that lift up or unplug for easy cleaning.

Make sure that you can get to the area underneath the coils to remove spilled foods.

Solid Element

What is it? Cast-iron discs that contain electric resistance wires embedded in ceramic insulation. Heat spreads evenly throughout element.

Pros: Sealed elements eliminate need for drip pans. Provide constant, even heat.

Cons: Slow to heat up and cool down. Requires perfectly flat bottom pan elements. Can absorb grease. This type is not self-cleaning, and the elements may rust unless properly maintained.

Buying tip: Look for thermostatically controlled elements that maintain preset temperature.

Ceramic-Glass: Radiant Element

What is it? High-speed radiant elements positioned beneath a smooth top surface. They transfer heat to the cookware by conduction and radiation.

Pros: Performance similar to that of electric coils but provides a smooth, clean look for modern kitchens. Good heat control and holds temperature well. Typically easy to clean and withstands high temperatures, extreme changes in temperature, and impact from heavy utensils. Most are stain resistant.

Cons: Requires flat-bottom pans that must fit element and not extend more than one inch over element edges for proper heating. Surface can stain if pan bottom and element are not clean before use. Sugary spills can pit surface if not wiped up before hardening.

Buying tip: Look for multiple-sized elements on the cooktop that accommodate small and large pans as well as a light that indicates when surface is hot. Patterned surfaces hide scratches fairly well.

Ceramic-Glass: Halogen Element

What is it? Quartz halogen lamp tubes that are encircled by electric resistance coils lie underneath the smooth cooktop surface, transfer heat to cookware.

Pros: Heat speed is faster than radiant. A smooth, clean look, good heat control, easy to clean, and withstands high temperatures and extreme changes in temperature as well as impact from heavy utensils. Stain resistant.

Cons: Element glows immediately when turned on, but heat response is no faster than radiant. This expensive surface can stain if pan bottom and element are not clean before use. Sugary spills can pit surface if not wiped up before hardening.

Buying tip: Look for at least one radiant element light that indicates when surface is hot, and a patterned surface to hide scratches.

Ceramic-Glass: Induction Element

What is it? Induction coil wires connected to solid-state controls are positioned under smooth top surface. Electric current to coils is converted into a high-frequency alternating current that flows through the coil and creates a magnetic field that generates heat in cookware made of magnetic materials.

Pros: Instant on/off heats up as fast as gas. It is the most energy efficient, as only the pot heats up—the stovetop surface remains relatively cool. Good for slow simmering and delivers smooth variable heat. High-tech clean look. Easy to clean and automatically shuts off if no pan is on cooktop (good safety feature) or if pan is smaller than 4 inches in diameter.

Cons: Very expensive and not widely available. All pans must be of a magnetic material.

Buying tip: Take your wallet!

Gas or Electric Downdraft Modular (Convertible) Cooktop

What is it? A variation of the basic gas or electric cooktop, but with interchangeable modules. Typically includes a grill with room for adding additional burners or cooking accessories such as a griddle, wok, or deep fryer.

Pros: Offers maximum flexibility in cooking, as it can be installed in a variety of locations such as in a center island or peninsula. Does not require a ceiling-mounted vent for grilling.

Cons: Expensive to purchase and install. Some of the components (grills, deep fryers, etc.) can be more difficult to clean.

Buying tip: Look for at least one high-powered burner, plus a smaller, low-powered burner and an easy-to-clean grill surface.

A CHECKLIST FOR FINDING A HOME FOR A RANGE (THIS WAS FURNISHED BY THE FOLKS AT SEARS)

❏ Assess your family's cooking and eating habits. Think about the types of food your family typically eats and how these foods are prepared.

❏ Determine the energy source that will fuel your range. The two options are gas or electric. Gas ranges require hookup to a gas line, and a 115-volt outlet for the lights and clock. Electric ranges need a 208- or 240-volt outlet. Unless you're building or remodeling, your choice may be limited to the existing energy source in your kitchen.

❑ Measure the space that's available for a range. Most free-standing ranges are 30 inches wide. Specialty ranges come in 20-, 24-, 36-, and 40-inch widths. Built-in ranges (either slide-in or drop-in models) are typically 30 inches wide, but come in other widths. Cooktops are also usually 30 inches, but come 36 inches wide. Wall ovens are 24, 27, or 30 inches wide.

❑ Determine a budget. Plan on spending at least $600 for an adequate freestanding gas range and $500 for an electric model. Built-ins, cooktops, and wall ovens will be considerably more pricey, with a slide-in range running at least $500. A cooktop and wall oven will cost more than an all-in-one range, averaging anywhere from $200 to $600 for a cooktop, and at least $600 for a good quality wall oven. Modular cooktops and dual or combination ovens will also add to the cost.

SALESMAN TECHNOSPEAK

- **Range:** Cooktop/oven combo features burners on top and an oven beneath.
- **Cooktop:** By itself this is half of your range—only the cooktop. Available in a variety of styles and heating elements, cooktops fit inside a precut hole in your countertop. The controls are usually mounted on top of the surface. You will need to buy a companion oven to complete the equation.
- **Wall oven:** Single or double-stacked oven that is built in to the wall.
- **Slide-in range:** This style range slides into your countertop and fits flush with the counter. Controls are usually mounted on the front of the range so it looks as if the oven and cooktop was built in to your cabinetry and countertop.
- **Downdraft ventilation cooktop:** Pioneered by Jenn-AIRE. As opposed to vents above the stove, this type of cooktop features air vents that suck the air downward out an escape vent. This type of ventilation is more effective than overhead hoods because the distance traveled is smaller, and they are typically quieter than overhead exhaust fans. Many downdraft ranges feature an intake fan, running down the center of the cooktop, that sucks in the air. This is the preferred method for cooktops that have burners as well as interchangeable grill tops and griddles.

- **Radiant oven:** Standard oven like a radiant cooktop features heated coils to cook food.
- **Convection oven:** This has a fan inside the oven portion of your range. Convection cooking uses fan-forced hot air to circulate inside the oven for faster cooking times and better browning of your meats and birds. Think TURBO!

SECTION II

A Collection of Cool Cooktops and Radical Ranges

Hot Radiant Cooktop: Kenmore's 36-Inch Radiant Cooktop Model No. 43645

$700

One of the hottest (pun intended) smooth-top electric cooktops around is Kenmore's new 36-inch model.

It features 5 electric-coil burners concealed beneath a uniquely patterned glass surface. Space age–style control knobs centered in the cooktop complement the unit's sleek design.

This stove performs like cooktops with electric coils but provides a smooth, clean look for the modern kitchen. It has good heat control and holds temperature well. It's also stain resistant, and will withstand high temperatures, extreme changes in temperature, and impact from heavy utensils.

Supersmooth Cooktop Range: Frigidaire's Gallery Professional Series Electric Range

$1,500

This radiant smooth cooktop features Frigidaire's exclusive Warm and Serve Zone—a low-wattage warming area between the 2 rear heating elements. The zone, which can accommodate a pot up to 9 inches in diameter, lets you keep cooked foods and soups warm (up to 170 degrees F.) without overcooking. This in turn frees the remaining 4 electric heating elements for actual cooking.

Below the cooktop is a convection oven (which uses fan-forced hot air to speed cooking times), as well as a unique warming drawer beneath the oven for keeping pastries, pies, and bread hot while you finish cooking. Other features include a built-in spice rack and a professional stainless steel design.

Hot Gas Cooktop: Thermador 36-Inch Black Glass XLO Cooktop

$1,219

One of the coolest-looking hot cooking surfaces on the market, this 36-inch drop-in cooktop features 5 gas burners on a stylish black glass cooktop. What's better is that two of its burners have a feature called XLO, which stands for "extra low." This feature provides the chef with a high degree of temperature control and accuracy for fragile foods like chocolate or butter. When activated, the XLO burner will actually shut off during its cycling process, allowing the heat of the burner top to slowly cook delicate foods or keep them warm until ready to serve. These burners virtually eliminate the need for double boiler pans used on most cooktops for slow cooking.

Other features include automatic ignition and reignition—no pilot lights required.

Best Gas Range: KitchenAid EasyConvect

$1,550

One of the most innovative new technologies to surface in the oven industry is convection cooking.

Convection ovens use fan-forced hot air to cook. The two main benefits to convection cooking are faster cooking times (a 5-hour turkey cooks in 3 hours) and lower energy costs. In addition, the end results are food that is juicier, crispier, and more evenly prepared.

The problem with most convection ovens is that they require different temperature and heat settings than standard radiant types. Calculating them can require the skill of an MIT graduate.

KitchenAid's new EasyConvect combines all the benefits of a gas cooktop with the speed of a built-in convection oven. The unit even simplifies convection recipe conversions—a computer chip automatically adjusts standard oven cooking times to convection times at the press of a button.

Best Induction Cooktop: Jenn-AIRE Designer Line Conventional Magnetic Induction and Ultra Quick-Start Radiant Cooktop

$800

This model combines 2 radiant electric and 2 induction elements side by side. Mixing two styles not only helps reduce the cost of the unit, it prevents you from having to throw away your aluminum pans.

Other features include a 30-inch cooktop, an audio "beep" on the induction elements that indicates when pans are positioned incorrectly, and a stylish, wipe-clean ceramic glass surface.

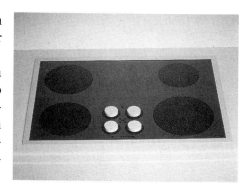

Portable Induction: Glowmaster Induction Cooker Model No. GMI 2000

$360

One way to experiment with induction cooking without tossing out your existing range and, for that matter, your pocketbook too is with this portable induction cooker from Glowmaster.

Great for buffets and tabletop cooking, or just a cooking companion, this 1,300-watt induction burner is 50 percent more powerful than butane stoves and nearly twice as fast as a standard cooktop cooking element. But what really makes this unit shine is its boil-to-simmer speed. Once the food item is boiled, this unit can, in less than 10 seconds, be reduced to a simmer setting without removing the pan from the cooktop. Truly a chef's dream, it features 3 electronic push button heat controls (Low, Medium, High—up to 450 degrees F.) and has a digital timer built-in as well.

SECTION III

Refrigerators

When we shop, although it may be a refrigerator's exterior cosmetics that pique our interest, it's what's on the inside that counts. Today's models are bursting on the inside with unique features like adjustable shelving, racks and shelves for 2-liter bottles and gallon jugs, and a plethora of other unique storage ideas that literally put those old cold boxes of yesteryear on ice.

There are four categories of refrigerators on the market:

- **Under mount:** A single-door unit with freezer underneath.
- **Top mount:** A single-door unit with the freezer above.
- **Side by side:** Half freezer, half refrigerator, one on each side.
- **Built-in:** Can be any type of refrigerator but is built in to the cabinetry.

Best Value Top Mount Refrigerator: Kenmore 24-Cu.-Ft. Refrigerator Model No. 4678592

$949

This 24-cubic-foot refrigerator features an icemaker and 4 adjustable slide-out tempered glass shelves for positioning taller items like 2-liter bottles and water pitchers. Measuring half the width of the refrigerator's interior, the shelves can be positioned at adjustable heights by connecting them to the interior wall mount in the refrigerator.

Other features include 2 large humidity-controlled crispers, 3 adjustable door bins with gallon jug storage, and a fold-out plastic grape and/or fruit holder.

Best Side-by-Side Refrigerator: Frigidaire's Gallery Series
$1,500

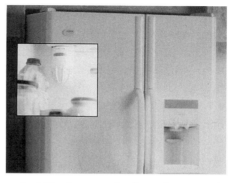

Other units may feature a chilled water and ice dispenser built into the door, but Frigidaire goes one step further by including a built-in replaceable cone-shaped water filter that reduces lead, chlorine, and bacteria levels in your ice and chilled water before they reach your glass. Each filter lasts approximately 6 months (replacements sell for $15) and includes a date indicator that reminds you when it's time to replace it. Not only does the dispenser deliver pure ice and water, it has a crushed-ice function as well.

Another unique feature is its "flip and slide" shelving, which allows you to flip a portion of the shelf and attach it to the inside wall of the refrigerator so you can easily store taller items such as two-liter soft drink or wine bottles.

Other features include gallon door bins, an insulated meat keeper bin that can be adjusted to different temperatures than the rest of the refrigerator, and spill-safe shelving (for Kelley) that holds spilled items on one shelf, preventing them from leaking or dripping all over the refrigerator.

SECTION IV

Dishwashers

Probably the best labor-saving device in your kitchen is the dishwasher. If you don't believe me, try not using it for a couple of weeks, and see how much you enjoy doing the dishes the old-fashioned way. A dishwasher is also efficient, as a typical, fully loaded dishwasher will use less water and detergent than doing the dishes by hand. Because of the pressure and water temperature generated, they also assist in keeping your plumbing clog-free.

The dishwasher is another appliance that has gone high-tech. Most new models feature computer chips with sensors for detecting dirt, new sprayer technology for more uniform cleaning, and larger tubs that allow for easy loading.

One of the biggest selling points on dishwashers today is noise reduction. While almost all new models feature some sort of insulation that reduces the churning and grunting sound of dishwashers, no two philosophies of noise reduction are alike. The technology we like best is the vent method, which combines insulation with a closed vent during wash cycles to virtually eliminate dishwasher noise.

Best-Value Dishwasher: Kenmore Ultra Wash

$300–$600

This dandy dishwasher features a sophisticated internal electronic sensor that detects high or low soil levels. It then automatically adjusts the wash cycle to either extend the wash or use less water, depending on load size.

Unlike other soil sensors, which detect the soil by analyzing the cloudiness of the water (and can be "fooled" by spilled milk or too much detergent), this model's sensor only adds a wash when soils or grease are actually present. Another benefit is its Automatic Temperature Control, which kicks in and adds heat to heavily soiled loads, and reduces the temperature when the load is not as dirty.

This machine has a lot of interior room too—enough for 12 place settings. And because it uses a three-level towerless spray system, there's more room for loading big pots and pans. There's also an insulated sound vent that closes during its cycle for superquiet operation.

Ultimate Dishwasher: Miele Integrated Dishwasher
$1,900

If money's no object, then check out this dishwasher from Miele. Okay, you've probably never heard of this manufacturer, but trust us, it's cool!

This state-of-the-art cleaning machine is invisible in your kitchen, as it is built into your cabinetry, with all its controls on the inside of the machine's door.

But don't let its stealth styling fool you—this unit is the ultimate cleaning machine. Integrated into the inside portion of the door are touch controls, which allow you, at the touch of a button, to begin a washing cycle that utilizes 3 spray arms, 3 filters, and a built-in water softener. Even better, the dishwasher has a unique full-width cutlery and silverware tray that slides out from the top and cradles all of your knives, forks, and spoons in an easy-to-load and -unload rack. In fact, the dishwasher has enough room to hold 14 place settings in one load—more than any other unit on the market.

Another unique feature is its Top Solo washing cycle for lighter loads, which conserves water and energy by concentrating the unit's spray only on the top cutlery tray and basket. Of course, this unit is whisper quiet—so you really won't know it's there.

Because we typically place larger pans facedown on the lower level of dishwashers, very little of the hot water directly reaches the glassware on the top shelf. The Miele has multiple spray arms (with one placed directly below the top rack), which ensures that every dish gets clean.

SECTION V

On the Waterfront

We don't want to gross you out, but according to the Centers for Disease Control, close to 20 confirmed new waterborne diseases break out each year. The culprit: aging water supply systems across the country. The bad news is that there's really no way to prevent diseases from forming in water supplies. Although chlorine and other chemical treatments help prevent major outbreaks of disease, they can also make water taste terrible. The good news is that many of the newer water purification systems not only eliminate the bad taste, they can get rid of the bad germs too.

While there are several types of water filtration systems on the market, many only remove chlorine and lead deposits, not harmful bacteria. The most common waterborne bacteria are called Cryptosporidium and Giardia. If you're looking for a water purifier for health purposes, not just for taste, make sure it is rated to remove these types of bacteria.

Here are a couple of our favorite new water purifiers.

Countertop Water Purifier: Sunbeam FreshSource Power Water Filtration System

$80

This one-of-a-kind electronic water dispenser rests on your countertop and delivers some of the cleanest and best-tasting H_2O around.

About the size of a coffeepot, the purifier consists of an AC-powered base station with a changeable filter cartridge that holds a ¾ gallon removable pitcher. To operate, simply fill the pitcher with water and place it on the base station. Electronic controls on top of the base unit allow you to press the container, soda fountain–style, against a panel and dispense water. For larger items like coffeepots, water bottles, and so on, the unit has an Auto Fill button for easy fillup.

The unit has an electronic filter watch light that tells you when to change the cartridge (about every 200 gallons, or after 6 months of usage—replacements sell for $15) and is rated to reduce up to 99 percent of the chlorine, lead, and harmful Cryptosporidium and Giardia bacteria from your water supply.

But the best part of this product is that it is simple to set up and use, so much so that the whole family can quickly get into the habit of using it.

Best Use of a Water Purification Product: Moen Pure Touch Faucet

$450

Until now the only way to get purified water directly from your sink was to attach one of those big bulky units over the screen of your faucet head—cumbersome devices that made it virtually impossible to do the dishes or fill stockpots underneath. This replacement faucet solves the add-on dilemma by incorporating a water filtration system inside the faucet itself. Of course you'll have to replace your existing faucet, a move that doesn't come cheap and often requires a plumber (depending on your confidence under the sink). Or you can spend $9.95 and purchase *The Gadget Guru's Make It Easy Guide to Home Repair* and learn how to replace a faucet yourself! (Okay, it's a shameless plug, but I'll guarantee that my publisher and editor will turn their heads when they read that line!) Nevertheless, this type of purifier makes a lot of sense.

The faucet features a built-in carbon block filter, made by water giant Culligan, that reduces chlorine, lead, and harmful bacteria like Cryptosporidium and Giardia in your drinking water. Each snap-in/out replaceable filter lasts for approximately 200 gallons of water or 3 months of usage (replacement filters sell for $23). The filter is monitored by a electronic LCD indicator located on the top of the faucet that alerts you both visually and audibly when it's time to change the filter. You can also switch the water supply to unfiltered for washing dishes and the like. But that's not all; this stylish faucet is tethered to a tube that allows it to be pulled away from the sink and used as a sprayer for cleaning vegetables or washing pots and pans.

This is possibly the most innovative product we've seen from Moen since our buddy Alan Pfenniger traveled from Cleveland to Nashville just to demonstrate Moen's polished brass fixture. Okay, that's not such a feat until you understand that he conducted this demonstration in the snow from the trunk of his car outside a restaurant after a late-night business dinner. Dedication? Too much single malt scotch? You be the judge! But we were so impressed that we put it in our newspaper column and on the *Today* show, and it even got a mention in this book. What a guy!

CHAPTER 6

The High-Tech Kitchen

As we've said before, the kitchen has become the family room of the 1990s. And you can bet that anywhere the crowd goes, the manufacturers of the world will follow. That's why names like Sony, RCA, and GE are appearing in cooks' nooks across the land.

Other than a telephone, which is a necessity in almost any room in the house, the television is the next most desirable product to have in the kitchen. But not just any television will do. Just imagine trying to cram that 35-inch set onto the countertop. That's why there are a plethora of under-the-cabinet models that are not only functional, but utilize what was once unused space. This trend was spawned from under-the-cabinet-mounted clock radios. So what's next? How about a VCR for the kitchen?

That's just the beginning; today's hot trend is computers for the kitchen. Not only am I editing this chapter while enjoying my morning cup of coffee, I am doing so on a computer that's located—yes, you guessed it—in the kitchen. When you stop and think about it, placing a computer in a kitchen makes sense. Not only can parents monitor children doing their homework while a meal is being prepared, but they can also use this strategically located computer to surf food-friendly websites to find new dinner recipes.

Even better, you can now go to Internet websites that allow you to avoid the long lines and crowded supermarket parking lots and do your grocery shopping online. This is truly the beginning of a new millennium.

So, whether it's listening to tunes, watching your favorite chef prepare a meal, grocery shopping, or downloading a recipe from a

CD-ROM or the Internet, this chapter will help you choose the right high-tech products for your kitchen.

SECTION I

Time and Tunes: A Selection of Kitchen Clocks, Radios, and CD Players

Whether you make pasta with Pavarotti, sauté with the Stones, or bake with Bach, a strategically located stereo makes a great addition to any kitchen.

The best part about kitchen audio products is that manufacturers understand there's no space for a bulky radio or a CD player, so they've created under-the-cabinet models that require little space and do not interfere with your countertop appliances.

Here are some of our favorites.

Best-Value Kitchen Clock Radio: GE Spacemaker Stereo Radio Cassette Player Model No. 7-4287

$80

You've probably heard of the Spacemaker line of kitchen products. GE developed this line of electronics for the kitchen years ago, and it has since become one of the most recognized and popular brands of electronic products for the kitchen. What separates the Spacemaker line from the pack is that its products are not just consumer electronics products painted white and marketed for the kitchen—they are built from the ground up for use in the kitchen. This truly makes a difference.

To prove our point, check out this GE Spacemaker under-the-cabinet-mounted cassette player, AM/FM stereo clock radio. Not only does it play your favorite tunes, its underside features a built-in lamp that illuminates the counter space below it. Even better, there's an extra appliance outlet on the back panel that's programmable—you can plug an appliance like a toaster or coffeemaker into the back and set the time you want it to come on. This is what I mean when I say that these items are designed specifically for the kitchen.

Other features include two 3-inch front-firing speakers, a large LED clock, and a front-loading cassette tray.

Best CD Clock Radio: Sony's CD/AM/FM Stereo Clock Radio Model No. ICF-CD533

$170

This cabinet-mount unit delivers the goods with a built-in AM/FM stereo, CD player, digital clock, and 2 powerful speakers with bass-rich sound. Even better, it has a wipe-clean membrane over its pushbutton controls to keep foods and sauces from seeping into the unit. (A peanut butter sandwich inserted into the VCR is one thing; spaghetti sauce on the radio tuner is another!)

Its clock is equipped with an AM/FM digitized stereo tuner and 5 station presets, which allow for one-button tuning. In addition, the unit features a 24-hour countdown timer with 5 memory presets for programming your cooking times or other time-monitored activities. It even has a self-power backup battery that keeps you from having to reset the clock after a power surge or loss.

Ultimate Kitchen CD Clock Radio: Proton CD/Stereo Clock Radio Model No. KS-530CD

$230

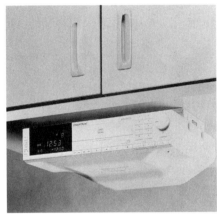

Further proof that the 1990s kitchen is getting the attention of consumer electronics manufacturers is evidenced by high-end audio/video equipment maker Proton's new under-the-cabinet-mount CD player/clock radio.

This compact all-white unit features 2 great-sounding 3-inch speakers, an electronic digital clock with LED display, front-loading CD player, and electronic frequency controls for precise tuning of your favorite radio talk show. (Some folks really do listen to Rush Limbaugh in the kitchen!)

But that's not all; this unit also has 20 electronic program presets and an intuitive On function that allows you to simply touch one of the station preset buttons for the unit to turn on automatically.

Besides its great sound, what really makes this a super kitchen companion is its built-in 2-hour countdown timer, which helps you keep track of cooking times so you don't burn the bundt cake.

SECTION II

TVs, VCRs, Phones, and More

I highly recommend a TV in the kitchen. Of course I may be a bit biased. I mean how else are you going to see those Gadget Guru segments on the *Today* show in the mornings?

Before you purchase a kitchen television, it's important to consider your needs. While some smaller units will mount under a cabinet, most are designed to rest on the countertop and can take the space once reserved for the stand mixer or coffeemaker. Another option is a TV/VCR combination unit. These are great for watching cooking videotapes or entertaining your youngster with *The Lion King* while you prepare dinner.

Also consider the antenna situation. If you don't have a cable hookup in the kitchen, make sure the television has an antenna that can be used in limited space. To make sure you can get reception from an antenna, test your kitchen by using your living room TV—sans cable. After you see the picture quality, or lack of it, you may want to call the cable company or satellite provider to add an outlet in the kitchen.

Of course, it's a requirement to set your kitchen's television dial to the *Today* show each day and truly see What a Difference Today Makes! Okay, enough with the commercials; here are some hot boxes, and some chatterboxes, for your kitchen.

Terrific Tiny Cabinet-Mount Color TV: GE Spacemaker 5-Inch AC/DC Color TV Model No. 05GP008

$230

Besides its compact size, what makes this 5-inch color television shine is its dual power capability. It mounts under the kitchen cabinet on a bracket and plugs in to an outlet, but this model also slides off easily and comes with a cigarette lighter adapter so you can take it to the ball game or camping, or place it in the car's backseat to keep your passengers entertained while traveling. Even better, it includes electronic signal-seek tuning for optimal reception.

It measures a mere 10×6×6.2 inches, and weighs a manageable 16 pounds. Other features include one set of earphone jacks, an audio/video input, and an antenna.

Best 9-Inch Color Kitchen TV: Sony's 9-Inch Cabinet-Mount Trinitron Model No. KV9PT50

$350

Although priced more like a microwave oven than a small television, this 9-inch color television delivers superior picture and sound quality. One of its best features is a unique swiveling bracket that allows you to watch from just about any angle in the kitchen, and a remote control that allows you to change channels or adjust the volume from just about anywhere too.

Other features include a sleep timer, one rear A/V input, a headphone jack, and a coiled cord control system that hides messy wires. It measures 10×10×12 inches and weighs 12 pounds.

Best TV/VCR for Your Kitchen: RCA KitchenVision Model No. T13070WH

$480

The best way to learn to cook is to watch somebody else do it. That's the idea behind the KitchenVision— a combination 13-inch color TV and built-in VCR.

Measuring just 15¾×14½×15 inches, this kitchen-white-colored TV/VCR combination unit features a built-in swivel and a remote control with a no-spill, wipe-clean protective membrane that promises to keep your secret spaghetti sauce off the electronics and in your favorite dish.

Its 2-head VCR features an 8-event/1-year programmable timer, auto head cleaner, and, best of all, an Italian cooking video titled *The de Medici Kitchen*, which includes numerous recipes on video that help get you started cooking in no time. You can also make your own videotape. Just take a camcorder over to your favorite chef's house (in my case that's my sister-in-law, Maria), videotape his/her cooking techniques, and play it back to duplicate the recipe. Or think about this idea for a wedding gift: You can videotape a variety of favorite family recipes and package them with this product.

Best Phone for Your Kitchen: GE Kitchen Phone

$60

GE's Kitchen Phone is the first telephone designed especially for use in the kitchen. Okay, almost any telephone can be wall-mounted and placed in the kitchen, but what separates this kitchen-white-colored model from the pack is that it features a membrane keypad that prevents your clam dip or chocolate sauce from damaging the phone. An extralarge speaker is also built in for hands-free conversations.

But the two things we like best about this phone are its extralong 15-foot tangle-free cord for easy maneuvering while you prepare meals and, most of all, the fact that somebody actually thought to put a call waiting button on the handset so you don't have to return to the base to see who's on the other line. This way, you'll never miss a lick when battering your shrimp.

Best Television Product to Make Coffee With: RCA's Home Director

$60

Couch potatoes will surely love this product—a remote control that allows them to take command of a television, VCR, cable box, lights, even a coffeemaker, all from the comfort of their easy chair.

From RCA comes the Home Director, which utilizes small modules to control just about any electrically powered device in the home.

Included in the kit are a base module and a remote control. The base module plugs into the wall; the power plug of a lamp or just about any electrical appliance can be plugged into it. Up to 15 additional modules or switches can be placed around the house. The modules are activated by the included UHF remote control. This control also operates your television, VCR, and cable box. The only restriction to its operation is that the remote has to be within 75 feet of the base module—but since the signal is UHF and can go around corners, the remote can be located behind a wall or in another room.

Each module has a specific code number; a lamp could be No. 3 and the coffeemaker No. 8. To operate, just press the remote's Home button, the corresponding module number, and On. This sends a radio signal to the base, which then sends a signal through your home's existing electrical wiring system, which tells that module to provide power to the unit. Even better, if the module is connected to a lamp, a press of a remote button commands it to dim or brighten.

To add more appliances, just install a separate module ($17) and assign it an unused number.

SECTION III

The Digital Kitchen

PC and Software for the Kitchen

You can run, but you can't hide; the digital revolution is about to invade the kitchen. Already major appliances like the dishwasher, stove, refrigerator, and microwave are incorporating microchips, but there's also an ever-growing category of new digital devices slowly pushing their way in. While some of them are literally pie in the sky—a topic we will embrace in the next chapter—others are readily available to the high-tech consumer.

This section peeks at the newest silicon chip–based devices for your kitchen, delves into the latest culinary software titles for your PC, and also takes a ride on the information superhighway for some of the hottest websites for the cooking crowd.

So put on your space suits and prepare to become aware of the digital delights available for your high-tech kitchen. Does the name Jetsons ring a bell?

Eclectic Electronic Kitchen Recipe/Shopping List Organizer: The Brother Kitchen Assistant

$200

If you're looking for an easy way to collect, organize, access, and store your recipes, then your ship has come in with this electronic kitchen device from the folks at Brother.

Like a computer in your kitchen, this modern-looking, countertop appliance takes up less space than a toaster and features a 7-line LCD black-and-white display screen and a reduced sized keyboard. It even has a built-in thermal printer.

Included in its memory are 75 family-oriented recipes that can be displayed with the press of a button. It also allows you to plan meals for the day or week, create shopping lists, and even search your recipe collection by selecting only those ingredients you have on hand. You can upgrade it too with additional slots for memory cards for holding your recipes or other titles.

Other features include 5 independent cooking timers, nutritional analysis, and an automatic scaling feature that instantly adjusts the recipe for a desired number of portions.

Its printer uses adding machine–sized (2¼-inches-wide) thermal paper that allows you to print shopping lists and recipes on demand. It operates on AA batteries or AC power (adapter included). Additional 32K (ROM) recipe cards with 120 preprogrammed recipes are $30, and 128K (RAM) memory cards that hold up to 150–200 of your personal recipes sell for $40.

World's Smartest Kitchen TV: The Kitchen Coach

$500

What Jane Fonda videos did for fitness at home, The Kitchen Coach hopes to do for aspiring cooks. That's because this revolutionary 3-in-1 color TV has a built-in CD player that not only plays music, but incorporates video CD technology that plays back special videos as well. The Kitchen Coach is like having your own culinary personal trainer with dozens of interactive instructional titles, all hosted by professional instructor/chefs and designed to make it easier to learn and prepare just about any type of food.

As opposed to videotape, video CDs are digital. This allows for more detailed information and graphics, menu screens, and crystal-clear freeze frames for stopping on a certain aspect of the lesson. What's more, the unit comes with a handy permeated remote control that makes it simple to navigate. Besides, how many VCRs can rewind from end to beginning in less than 5 seconds?

The Kitchen Coach System includes a 9-inch color TV, a built-in video CD player, and 6 video CDs with interactive step-by-step video demonstrations. They are: Master Chefs Secrets, The Fundamentals, Classic Accomplishments, Essential Techniques, Lowfat and Healthful, and The 30-Minute Gourmet. There are currently more than 15 video CD titles available for The Kitchen Coach.

Allow me to note that The Kitchen Coach folks are not resting on their laurels. In January 1999, they are expected to preview The WebCoach TV, a Kitchen Coach with a built-in modem and Internet browser featuring shopping links to grocery, meats, wine, and other kitchen products, a printer port, and a video conferencing phone link as well.

CD-ROM COOKBOOKS

Today's electronic CD-ROM cookbooks are more than just large databases of recipes. They offer a wealth of information no conventional cookbook can even come close to delivering. Where else but on a CD-ROM can you create and print shopping lists and recipe cards, scale recipes for the number of servings necessary, get nutritional analysis, enter your own recipes, and watch video tips of the pros preparing your favorite foods.

In fact, next to Quicken for finances and kids' educational titles, a cookbook on CD-ROM is a must-have for any computer owner.

Here are some of our favorites.

Best Overall Electronic Cookbook: Williams Sonoma Guide to Good Cooking

$40

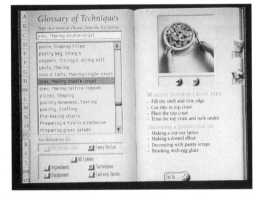

What do you get when you combine the cyber knowledge of the Brøderbund Company and the gourmet food knowledge of Williams Sonoma? You get this awesome cooking CD-ROM loaded with tips, recipes, and tons of other information to make a great cook out of even the most marginal kitchen inhabitant.

What we like best about this CD-ROM is that it's easy to use. We see way too many cooking software titles bogged down with confusing indexes, hard-to-find recipes, and complicated menus that are so confusing that they can take your appetite away. This CD-ROM features 1,000 recipes complete with graphic color photographs of kitchen items you need, a video library of cooking tips and techniques, and an easy-to-navigate recipe finder. Even better, it has over 60 video clips with step-by-step video directions and a menu planner that allows you to create your own menus from the recipe list and save them for later use.

For the mathematically challenged (like us), this package includes a scaling program that allows you to convert the recipe ingredients to the number you have to feed—no calculator needed. However, the only function missing is the ability to add your own recipes to this program. Maybe the next generation will include this feature. For a great recipe insertion program, see Mangia below.

Best Cooking Software for Adding Your Own Recipes: Mangia

$20

If you're looking for a kitchen software title that allows you to learn new recipes as well as allowing you to enter your own favorite concoctions, then check out Mangia. With more than 800 recipes and an expandability feature, it is one of the best virtual cookbooks on the market today.

This electronic cookbook makes meal planning, recipe selection, even grocery shopping easier than ever. Mangia features an intuitive search engine that can locate recipes by ingredients, cooking times, difficulty, course, or nationality. It allows you to print recipe cards, pages, and booklets using its bundled fonts and professionally designed formats—you can even create your own cookbook.

Mangia also includes scaling capabilities, which allow you to enter the number of people eating and automatically have the amount of ingredients you need displayed on-screen. There's also a nutritional analysis meter with low-fat substitutions. Shopping lists are simplified too, as the program automatically omits ingredients you already have in your pantry and can even organize this list into ingredients by the section of the store where they are found, saving you shopping time. Now that's a cool feature!

Best Chefs on an Electronic Cookbook: Multicom's Great Chefs Great Cities

$15

Based on the popular PBS series Great Chefs Great Cities, this CD-ROM takes you on a journey to more than 17 cities around the country for an in-depth look at their gourmet kitchens and includes 30 minutes of video tips and techniques. The software also includes 290 recipes.

As a bonus feature, this software package also comes bundled with a cookbook titled *The Louisiana New Garde Cookbook*, featuring 115 recipes from the hottest cooking region of the country, as well as 100 subrecipes for delicious sauces, seasonings, and stuffings from the likes of Emeril Lagasse, owner of New Orleans's famed Emeril's restaurant.

Best Kitchen Design Software: Autodesk Picture This Home

$50

Another great way to use your computer to enhance your kitchen lifestyle is with a kitchen design program. Like an architect in a box, a kitchen design program will help you remodel without leaving the comfort of your home, and without emptying your wallet.

The problem with most in-home design software we've seen is that it's too complicated. This new software from Autodesk, however, is relatively easy to use. It not only allows you to visualize and plan a new kitchen before investing time and money, it has a one-of-a kind shopping database filled with thousands of real images of real products from more than 30 different manufacturers. This allows you to literally drag and drop an appliance from its shopping mode and place it in the rendering you've developed. JPEG thumbnail photographs of everything from the latest cooktops, wall ovens, ranges, refrigerators, cabinetry, doors and windows, plumbing, floors, and countertops to wall coverings are included in the shopping area. Even if you don't want to design your kitchen, the shopping database is worth the price of admission because it is so full of items from companies like GE, KitchenAid, Armstrong, and Whirlpool that it makes a great catalog for selecting the right appliances and materials.

Other features include a 3-D plan for a quick start—choose one of the five most common layouts—a Decorate mode that allows you to add color, even curtains, to your design, a budget calculator with a project worksheet, and a Compare function that allows you to save a file and compare and contrast it with up to four other layouts that you've saved.

SECTION IV

A Culinary Travel Guide to the Information Superhighway

The Internet is an awesome resource for cooks. Not only can you find great recipes and tips, but most major manufacturers have also uploaded entire lines of products so you can let your fingers do the walking and shop from the comfort of your home—no persistent salesmen allowed. For the thrifty cook, clipping coupons on the Net is also much easier than scouring the Sunday paper.

This section is a collection of our favorite sites along the Information Superhighway. It will help you surf to the best soufflé, click on a perfect pasta recipe, and ally with a new appliance manufacturer. So let's boot up and wander through the Net.

GADGET GURU'S TOP 10 FOOD SITES ON THE INTERNET

1. http://www.gadgetguru.com We'd be remiss if we didn't recommend our own website. It is updated daily with the latest and greatest products from consumer electronics to housewares, hardware, sporting goods, and everything in between. Our site is full of links to manufacturers and, like this book, offers helpful reviews and tips on anything new. Check us out on America Online, too. Keyword: Gadget.

2. www.netgrocer.com Definitely the wave of the future, NetGrocer is the first nationwide online supermarket offering thousands of name-brand items at prices up to 20 percent lower than supermarket prices. By shipping directly from their warehouse they cut out the middleman and pass the savings on to you. They will ship your order via FedEx for only $2.99 for orders up to $50 ($4.99 for orders over $50). A guaranteed delivery date (1–4 business days) will be given to you once you submit your order, and you can track your order from their customer service area. Make sure you get on their mailing list, as you will receive information on special sales via e-mail.

3. www.foodsafety.org This is a multistate/agency effort toward a sustainable system of national food safety databases. The primary funding agency is the United States Department of Agriculture. A great place to learn about proper food handling and foodborne diseases.

4. www.butterball.com Never cooked a turkey? This site, featuring the Butterball University, will have you baking a bird in no time. Fun and informative, this site is a must see.

5. http://starnews.webpoint.com/food/shguru.htm This informative website is produced by our friend Phil Lempert, who also appears periodically on the *Today* show. Phil analyzes the food marketing industry to keep consumers up-to-date about cutting-edge marketing trends and new food products.

6. http://www.kitchenlink.com This website features more than 7,500 cooking-related links full of recipe tips and just about anything else you can think of for cooks to do.

7. www.almanac.com Updated daily, this site is full of useful kitchen tips and recipes. It'll help you grow you own food too.

8. www.kraftfoods.com This cheesy site has not only information on cheese, but lots of helpful tips and techniques on just about any culinary subject. There are coupons and recipes too.

9. http://www.kidsfood.org Get the little ones interested in the food they eat with this informative and educational site. Fun for the whole family.

10. http://www.crazyveg.com Let the crazy vegetarian turn you on to turnips and other green delights. Definitely a fun site to take a look at.

CHAPTER 7

Crystal Ball

While we've featured futuristic products throughout the book, they've got nothing on the products of tomorrow.

The best thing about writing a chapter about the kitchen of the future is that we can make everything up—there's no way for you to find out if we are right or wrong. Only time will tell. But, because all we do is test new products for a living, we do have good insights on what the future will yield. So enjoy this chapter with the understanding that fact is stranger than fiction and that in the future, the Jetsons will seem like the Flintstones.

I know it's become a cliché, but the digital revolution is rapidly changing just about everything we do. Take the computer, for example. The average life span of a new computer technology is six months—six months! Remember, it took the microwave guy two decades to create a microwave for the consumer market. For that matter, it took centuries for someone to figure out how to roast coffee beans.

Years ago, at a housewares trade show, Sharp Electronics showed the freezer of the future. Of course, in reality, it was just a mockup that did not work, but Sharp predicted that you would take your leftovers and place them in the flash freezer department, and they were frozen solid in under a minute. Although it was only a speculative demonstration, this type of product will most likely become reality in the near future. When you think about it, a flash freezer for the kitchen makes sense. It works like a microwave in reverse; instead of quickly heating foods, you can immediately freeze them. This way, you can eliminate just about any chance of spoilage while preserving your leftovers with a minimum of fuss. When products such as this one make it to reality, the kitchen as we know it today will seem almost unbelievably quaint and nostalgic.

SECTION I

Future Products

The Hub of the Home: IBM's Family Message Center

Sure, we've all heard of home control devices that will control your house's lighting, appliances, telephone, e-mail, and fax messages, but what about technology that not only automatically accumulates a shopping list, but helps you decide what's for dinner?

That's the idea behind IBM's Family Message Center. This product features a voice-activated and touch-controlled computer screen built in to your cabinet that acts as the hub of a variety of activities. Its main feature is a cabinet-mounted bar code scanner device (like those at grocery stores) that allows you to scan food items to keep a household inventory. So, when you're unpacking the groceries, just pass them in front of the scanner, and they're entered into memory. If you're ever concerned about an item's freshness date, not to worry, since the computer knows when you purchased it, and knows when it expires. When you are finished with a particular item, before you throw it in the recycling bin, you scan it and the computer will put it on your shopping list. Even better, if you can't decide what to cook for dinner, simply scan a few items from the pantry, and it will give you a list of recipes (from an electronic cook-book or from an Internet site) based on what you have on hand.

What's more, because the unit is connected to the Internet you can have it automatically search the Net for coupons and print them out, or (remember, we are in the future here) have the computer automatically comparison-shop, order your food directly, and schedule delivery.

What's even more impressive about this vision of the future is that while it's not available to the public, working models have been shown at trade expositions. In fact, last year IBM demonstrated a Family Message Center in the Cyber Home 2000 display in San Francisco.

THE KITCHEN TABLE COMPUTER

In the future, instead of your having a computer on the kitchen table, the kitchen table could incorporate or even become a computer. Imagine having computing activities such as your Windows environment, with icons for games, communication, reference materials, and so on, projected onto the wall. Well, that's what IBM is trying to make happen. So that it could be operated by multiple users simultaneously, each family member would have a separate handheld flat panel device that could pull information off the main unit and download to a personal information device. Family members would be able to work on individual projects—reading news, making travel plans, playing games, or whatever—without having to wait for another user to complete a project.

Flexible Folding Video Screen

So what type of screen is your kitchen computer going to project upon? How about this RCA future-brand folding Flex Screen? This concept features a paper-thin screen and handheld remote control that folds up when not in use. Video

footage would be stored on holographic memory chips, which would hold incredible amounts of data.

Mirror Mirror

Another screen possibility? How about the Mirror Mirror from RCA? This prototype television is built in to a mirror. It combines a TV image inside that can be reduced or expanded to fill the mirror frame. Hey, you can watch the Guru on NBC while shaving. Now that's a scary thought!

Ceran's Cook-In—a Twenty-first Century Vision

This futuristic cooking apparatus from Schott industries, makers of the popular Ceran smoothtop cooking surface, projects a kitchen without pots and pans, a stovetop, cutting boards, or even the kitchen sink.

The 6-foot-long Cook-In table replaces traditional sinks and stovetops and uses a concave Ceran panel as both a cooking surface and sink. Each surface can be sectioned off with waterproof dividers, creating a series of cleaning or cooking wells that can be designated hot or cold and placed side by side. Fitted cutting boards can be inserted so veggies can be cleaned, chopped, and cooked within inches of each other. The Cook-In's water system is located—believe it or not—overhead. Its exhaust vent contains hoses that you pull down to the desired area.

Imagine a kitchen without cookware—what would we do with all the room?

The Microwave Dryer

Imagine being able to dry your clothes as fast as it takes to make a microwave meal! The folks at the Electronic Power Research Institute (EPRI) have produced such a device. Appropriately called The Microwave Dryer, this unit not only will save energy, it'll save your clothes too. No more shrinkage because the temperatures are too hot. In fact, in tests, microwave clothes dryers have completely dried the clothes at just 98 degrees F. as opposed to conventional dryers, which heat to 160 degrees F. (which can damage clothing). The water is heated and dried from the clothes by the microwaves, not by the warm clothes' tumbling over one another.

EPRI is working on a solution so that metals won't damage the unit. So far, they say the dryer can handle a small amount of metal, like zippers and buttons on pants or denim jackets. But there is a bit of a snafu when it comes to someone leaving metals in their pockets, for example, nails and bobby pins. They have, however, installed a safety sensor that will detect a hot metal object and turn the unit off to prevent damage.

SECTION II

Products We'd Like to See in the Future

- A coffeepot that doesn't spill when you pour. You'd be surprised how many coffeepots dribble when you pour a cup.
- A toaster with a self-cleaning crumb tray. Maybe it can be vacuumed out through the wall?
- A true self-cleaning stove. (Note to manufacturers: High heat is NOT self-cleaning.)
- Kitchen floors that clean themselves. Tiny holes like an air hockey table that suck dirt away. Maybe they could change colors too.
- A self-unloading dishwasher. Forget all the technologies inside a dishwasher; how about helping us unload it too?
- A see-through stove. Let's face it, we like to see things cook. Make us a clear range we can see inside, so we don't have to peer through a small window.
- Virtual recipe books. Images that float in midair—like a hologram above the cooking area. This would be the ultimate hands-free cookbook, as the pages would never stick together with remnants of spaghetti sauce.

Compendium A
Kitchen Safety

After the bathroom, the kitchen is the second most dangerous room in the house. Eighty-five percent of house fires begin there, and for children the kitchen is like a minefield. Here's a quick safety primer:

SAFETY TIPS

- All electrical appliances and tools should have a testing agency label.
- Unplug electrical appliances when not in use, and coil the cords so the little ones can't pull them off the counter.
- Have appliances repaired immediately if they aren't working properly.
- Don't overload the outlets.
- Water and electricity combined cause shock.
- Have dry hands; don't stand in water.
- If an appliance gets wet, have it serviced.
- Don't store things over the stove.
- Wear tight sleeves when you cook. Loose-fitting garments can catch fire.
- Smoke alarms should be in the kitchen, as well as in other rooms throughout the house.
- Fire extinguishers should be in the kitchen, as well as in other rooms throughout the house.
- Don't throw water on grease fires; use an extinguisher that you keep close at hand.
- Check the expiration date on your extinguisher.

- Keep a first-aid kit in the kitchen.
- Test your microwave for leakage (kits are available at hardware and home stores).

SECTION I

Fire Extinguishers Can Save Your Life and Your Home

You should have working and properly maintained ABC-type fire extinguishers in the kitchen, basement, garage, utility room, and anyplace else the possibility of fire exists. They should be hung on their brackets and placed near doorways on unblocked areas of the wall. Everyone in your family who is capable of understanding how to use them should know where they are.

What's important to understand here is that no one should ever be a hero. You can prepare yourself to handle small fires effectively, but if at any moment things seem to be getting out of control, leave the house and call the fire department. Staying is not worth the risk.

Here's what you need to know about fire extinguishers, how to operate them, and how to use them on common small fires.

RATINGS

- **Class A:** Designed for wood, paper, rubber, and many plastics.
- **Class B:** Designed for oil, solvents, grease, gasoline, kerosene, and other flammable liquids. Class B extinguishers are filled with dry chemicals.
- **Class C:** Designed for electrical fires. Class C extinguishers are also filled with dry chemicals.

➤**Tip:** The people who make fire extinguishers have also come up with a so-called multipurpose type, or ABC, which can be used to fight most small fires in the home. I recommend the ABC type because if there's an emergency you don't have to think about which extinguisher to grab.

BUYING AND USING A FIRE EXTINGUISHER

- Look for a fire extinguisher in the 2½- to 7-pound range. It's extremely important that you follow the manufacturer's recommendations for longevity of the unit and read the pressure gauge to make sure it's within the recommended range. After all, fire extinguishers are no good if they don't work.
- Read the instructions carefully so that you know how to use a fire extinguisher before the need arises. They all operate in essentially the same way. First, be sure that the fire isn't between you and an exit in case you have to leave in a hurry. Pull the pin or other release mechanism.
- Aim at the base of the fire and sweep from side to side until the fire is out.
- Stand about 6 to 10 feet away from the fire and near an exit. Pull the release mechanism and spray in a side-to-side motion at the base of the flames. The fire may seem to grow before it starts to go out. If flames get scattered by the spray, move back and extinguish them as well. Keep spraying until the fire is out and then watch carefully to make sure it doesn't flashback (start again).
- If the fire is electrical, shut off the main service panel after you've extinguished the fire and call the fire department.

HOW TO PUT OUT A KITCHEN FIRE

How to Put Out a Fire in a Pan

- Don't move the pan.
- Turn off the burners and the fan in the range hood if it's on.
- Put on an oven mitt or protect your hand with a hot pad. Slide the lid of the pan, or a platter that is larger than the diameter of the pan, over it to smother the flames. It's important to slide the covering over the fire, because if you pop it on top the flames may spread.
- If the flames persist, pour baking soda on the fire. Once it's out, let the pan cool before removing it from the stove.

How to Put Out a Fire on the Stovetop

- If the fire has spread from the pot to the stovetop, don't move the pan or pot.
- Turn off the burners and the range fan.
- Pour baking soda generously on the fire until it's extinguished. If baking soda doesn't do the job use a fire extinguisher.

➤**Tip:** Never put water, flour, or baking powder on a stovetop fire—it will only spread the flames.

How to Put Out a Fire in the Oven

- If you have a fire in the oven, closing the oven door and turning off the oven can sometimes put it out. This shuts off the supply of oxygen.
- If that doesn't work, you'll have to go to the fire extinguisher.

SECTION II

Gas and Carbon Monoxide

Gas

- In its natural state the gas we use to run our appliances is odorless and colorless; you'd never know it was there until it was too late. The odor we smell is added by the utility company to let us know there's a problem.
- If you smell gas in a room, shut off any flame and open windows to clear the fumes. Don't touch switches or unplug appliances from outlets—a spark could set off an explosion. Once the room is clear, consult the appliance's manual for information on relighting pilot lights if any are out.
- If the odor remains, or if you come home and smell gas, gather

your family and **LEAVE THE HOUSE IMMEDIATELY.** Call the utility company from a neighbor's phone, and don't go back inside until the problem is fixed.

➤**Tip:** This is how you shut off the gas supply to an appliance: The valve that controls the flow of gas to your stove or water heater works on the same principle as a plumbing supply valve. It should be located nearby, on the pipe that feeds the appliance. Turn the handle perpendicular to the gas pipe to shut off the gas. The main gas valve will be located at the gas meter. Keep a pair of channel locks nearby to turn the handle perpendicular to the main gas pipe.

Carbon Monoxide

- The fumes that come from any combustible source (wood, gas, kerosene, and the like) contain carbon monoxide. Breathing carbon monoxide for an extended length of time can cause serious illness and even death.
- It's important to vent everything properly and keep all vents and ducts clean and free of debris.
- Have your chimney and heating system inspected yearly.
- Companies like First Alert make carbon monoxide detectors that sense its presence the same way smoke detectors sense smoke.

➤**Tip:** Inside your home, never use charcoal, propane, or wood-burning grills intended for use outdoors. There is no venting for the fumes, and you are vulnerable to carbon monoxide poisoning.

➤**Tip:** If you own a gas stove, never use aluminum foil to line your oven or burners because it impedes combustion and can cause carbon monoxide to build up.

Kitchen Fire Extinguisher: The Flamestop

$13

Eighty-five percent of all house fires start in the kitchen. The Flamestop is specially formulated with a nontoxic wetting agent, which smothers the vapor, thus preventing the fire from burning without a big mess or destruction of surrounding areas. Each 16-ounce canister is much lighter than a bulky traditional fire extinguisher and has an easy-to-control spray handle like that on an aerosol can, which can be sprayed from any direction.

Combination Carbon Monoxide/Smoke Detector: First Alert

$50

Although every house should have a carbon monoxide detector and smoke alarm, if you have a gas stove, put a carbon monoxide detec-

tor in your kitchen. Why? Because carbon monoxide is a toxic, possibly deadly, tasteless, odorless, colorless gas and can be a by-product of an improperly installed or nonfunctioning gas kitchen range or cooktop vent.

A great space saver and lifesaver too, this combination alarm features two different tones and two lighted icons for distinction between smoke and carbon monoxide alarms. It is powered by a 9-volt battery and has a testing mode as well.

SECTION III

Kids' Safety

KIDS IN THE KITCHEN (CHECKLIST)

❏ Keep all cleaners out of cabinets, even the ones that kids have to climb up to. Best advice is to lock them up.

❏ Use cookware with cool-touch handles to prevent children from grabbing hot pots when you're cooking.

❏ Turn pot handles when you cook so children can't pull them down.

❏ Cover unused electrical outlets and appliances.

❏ Store knives, food processor blades, and other sharp objects in an unreachable place or lock them up.

❏ Look for small appliances, microwaves, and coffeemakers with child safety locks or auto off functions.

❏ Never leave the kitchen unattended while you cook. It only takes a second for accidents to happen.

❏ When you bake, make sure your child stays away from the oven.

❏ Keep the poison control number posted on your refrigerator.

Compendium B
Simple Appliance Repairs

Whether you just purchased a new appliance or want to keep your existing unit in tiptop shape, here are some handy repair tips to keep them running. You may even save a few bucks!

SECTION I

Drains and Traps

Fixing Clogs and Leaks

I'm a big believer in trying the easiest thing first, and when it comes to clogs there's nothing easier than starting with this trusty plumber's helper.

PLUNGING 101

Take out the drain plug and/or strainer. Place the plunger over the drain opening and run cold water until it covers the plunger cup. This helps create the necessary vacuum. Move the plunger up and down rapidly and with short even strokes. It might take a while, so don't give up too soon. If that doesn't work, then try this:

UNCLOGGING A SINK TRAP DRAIN

Sometimes what stops up a drain is debris in the trap that hasn't made its way to the line. The trap is the first thing you pull apart when you go after a clog.

You'll need: channel lock pliers, a wire brush, a plastic bucket, rubber gloves, and an old towel (to put under the bucket; it saves on cleanup).

• Put the bucket under the trap to catch the water and whatever else it's holding. Loosen the slip nuts with channel lock pliers. When they are loose they will slide away from the connections.

• Pull the trap from the connections and dump it into the bucket. Use the wire brush to clean out any sticking debris. If necessary, take the trap to another sink and flush it with hot water. Reassemble and run water to check for leaks.

➤**Tip:** Here's the best reason of all not to use caustic drain cleaners: If your drain is really clogged, no drain cleaner, caustic or otherwise, will free it. That leaves one alternative. You or somebody else is going to have to remove the sink trap to work on it. What's the problem? The trap is going to be full of drain cleaner just waiting to spill out when you take the trap apart. And believe me, that stuff burns. For the record, the use of liquid cleaners more often than not can be considered temporary, not a permanent fix.

SECTION II

Fix the Fridge

REPAIRING AND MAINTAINING YOUR REFRIGERATOR

We really have to remember that things were never intended to last forever, and no matter how bulky and solid a refrigerator or freezer may seem, it's like everything else—occasionally it needs a little love, affection, and personal attention.

To keep your refrigerator in good condition:

- At least once, but preferably twice a year, clean the condenser coils. They're located either underneath or behind the unit. Use the crevice tool on your vacuum cleaner to suck out the dust and anything else that may have found its way back there.
- Clean the gaskets (the piece of rubber that goes around your refrigerator door) around the refrigerator frequently to remove food particles. (Do the same with your dishwasher.)

LEVELING YOUR REFRIGERATOR

Modern refrigerators have leveling screws or legs in the front. It's important that the refrigerator be level for it to work properly.

You'll need a screwdriver, a carpenter's level, and a block of 2×4 pine.

- Check the unit with the level on the front and on the side. The refrigerator should be plumb (vertical) on the side. While setting the unit to tip slightly front to back, make sure the doors stay closed, because an open door can also adversely affect the operation of an icemaker.
- If the legs are adjusted with screws, use your screwdriver to raise or lower them until the unit is sitting properly.
- If the legs adjust by screwing, the fastest way to level the unit is to tilt it back and place a block of wood underneath to hold it up while you turn the leveler legs. (Counterclockwise will raise the unit; clockwise will lower it.) Make adjustments until it's level.

REPLACING A REFRIGERATOR DOOR GASKET

If you see no obvious cracks or tears in the gasket but still suspect that it's not sealing properly, there are two ways to see if it needs replacement:

- Take a dollar bill and close the door on it. There should be a little resistance when you pull it out.

- Put a work light with a wattage of 100 to 150 inside the compartment. Close the door and look around the seal for light leaks. If you see light, it's time to replace the gasket.

  A door gasket is easy to replace as long as you do it in steps. After you've replaced the gasket, a good maintenance idea is to rub the gasket with a little mineral oil. It'll keep the gasket flexible and make it less likely to crack. Replacing a dishwasher gasket is a similar process.

  You'll need a screwdriver or nut driver, and an exact replacement gasket.
- Soak the replacement gasket in warm water to make it more flexible and easier to work with. Unplug the refrigerator.
- Start at the top of the door and loosen (don't remove) the retaining screws or nuts. Slip the old gasket out, and slide the new one in. Retighten the screws. Move to the side and repeat the process all around the door.

FIXING SAGGING DOORS

Eventually refrigerator doors will start to sag—it's just a gravity thing. When they do, they start to cost you money because the seal is compromised and cold air escapes, making the unit work harder to keep food cold.

To fix a sagging door, you'll need a screwdriver or nut driver.

- Gently pry off the plastic cap with the screwdriver. Use the screwdriver to tighten screws or nuts.
- Lift the door from the end as you tighten.
- If the freezer and refrigerator have separate doors, you'll have to remove the freezer door in order to get to the refrigerator door.

SECTION III

Dishwasher Troubleshooting

DOESN'T FILL

- Sounds simple, but make sure the water is turned on.
- Check the float and see if anything is clogging the opening.
- Check the inlet screen valve to see if it's clogged.

DOESN'T DRAIN

- See if the drain filter, strainer, pump, or drain valve is clogged.
- Make sure the drain hose isn't looped or kinked.

DOESN'T CLEAN

- Use a meat thermometer to make sure the water is hot enough (130 to 140 degrees F.). Hold it under the hot water faucet to get a reading.
- Check for clogs and make sure the detergent dispenser is not gummed up, which prevents it from releasing soap. Dishwashing detergent also tends to get hard and lumpy when it gets old.

CHANGING HOSES

If hoses are cracked and hard they need to be replaced.

- Buy exact replacements and save the worn ones so you can use them as models to cut the new ones to the proper length with a mat knife.
- Most hoses are attached to appliances with spring clips. Put on a pair of safety goggles and get your pliers. Squeeze the prongs of the clip with the pliers, and slide it off the coupling.

- Remove the hose and replace it.
- If the hose is stuck, slit it with a utility knife and peel it away.

FIXING LEAKS

- Check the gasket on the dishwasher door to be sure it's in good shape.
- Look for clogs in the inlet and outlet valves.
- Check that the seal on the pump is good.
- Make sure the clamps on the hoses are tight.

➤**Tip:** Here's the way to prevent leaks and pump failures in your dishwasher. After the dishwasher's cycle, a certain amount of water remains in the bottom. Why? To keep the seals and O-rings moist and therefore to protect the seal. If the water evaporates, the seals dry up, the pump could freeze, and leaks might follow. If you're not using the dishwasher for an extended period, pour a little mineral oil in the bottom. The oil will float on top of the water and prevent it from evaporating.

Special Thanks

Writing a book is a huge undertaking, and without the help of many around us it simply would not be possible.

We'd especially like to thank the folks in the housewares industry for their input and expertise. They include the folks at Lamson knives and Chicago Cutlery, The Myer Cookware Corporation for all the help with cookware (thanks to Gretchen Holt especially), Ekco housewares for their bakeware support, and the folks at Progressive housewares as well. Then there's Mary Rogers of Cuisinart, and Bryan Maynard and Don Stuart at Frigidaire.

We'd especially like to thank Ann Wolman at Sears Kenmore for her help in deciphering all the categories of ranges, refrigerators, and stoves.

Thanks as well to Phil Lempert (the Supermarket Guru) for his insight, Randy Rayburn for his culinary knowledge, and all the recipe donors who took time to share their favorite concoctions with us.

Manufacturers' Telephone Numbers

CHAPTER 1: KITCHEN ESSENTIALS

Artex: (800) 521-0505
Bagel Biter: (800) 462-9237
Bemis: (800) 558-7651
Chef'n: (800) 426-7101
Chef'sChoice/Edgecraft: (800) 342-3255
Chicago Cutlery: (800) 545-4411
Ekco: (800) 367-3526
EMSA: (800) 827-2582
Fats Off: (800) 927-5356
Food Buddy: (888) 644-6603
Frieling: (800) 827-2582
KitchenArt: (800) 239-8090
Krups: (800) 526-5377
Lamson: (800) 872-6564
MagicKan: (888) 259-7772
Metro: (800) 367-0845
Misto: (888) OIL SPRAY
Norcross: (800) 223-6212
OXO: (800) 445-6836
Progressive: (800) 426-7101
Safety Can, The: (800) 999-6595
Seasonart: (800) 217-1958
SnapWare: (800) 334-3062
Soehnle: (800) 827-2582
Tuckers: (800) STOP BURNS
Yaffa: (800) 800-0073

CHAPTER 2: COOKWARE

All-Clad: (800) ALL-CLAD
Artex: (800) 521-0505
Auto Chef: (800) 217-1958
Calphalon: (800) 809-PANS
Circulon: (800) 326-3933
Corning Ware: (800) 999-3436
Double Decker Baking Rack: (800) 990-RACK
Farberware: (718) 863-8000
Intelligent Lid: (800) 217-1958
Joyce Chen: (978) 671-9500
Kuhn Rikon: (800) 662-5882
Max Burton: (800) 272-8603
Metro: (800) 367-0845
Metrokane: (800) 724-4321
Pan Companion: (800) 799-PANS
Progressive: (800) 426-7101
Pyrex: (800) 999-3436
T-Fal: (201) 575-1060
VillaWare: (800) 822-1335
Wear-Ever: (800) 527-7727

CHAPTER 3: COUNTERTOP APPLIANCES

Amana: (800) 843-0304
Black & Decker: (800) 231-9786
Bodum: (800) 232-6386
Braun: (800) 272-8611
Capresso: (800) 767-3554
Cuisinart: (800) 726-6247
Gino's: (800) 233-9054
Hamilton Beach: (804) 273-9777
Kenmore: (847) 286-8309
KitchenAid: (800) 422-1230
KitchenArt: (800) 239-8090
Krups: (800) 526-5377
Melitta: (813) 535-7376

Mr. Coffee: (800) MRCOFFEE
Oster: (800) 621-8854
Salton: (800) 272-5629
Samsung: (800) 933-4110
Sanyo: (818) 998-7322
Sharp: (800) BE SHARP
Starbucks Barista: (800) STARBUC
SwissMar: (800) 387-5707
T-Fal: (201) 575-1060
Toastmaster: (800) 947-3744
VillaWare: (800) 822-1335
Welbilt: (800) 872-1656
West Bend: (414) 334-2311
Zojirushi: (800) 733-6240

CHAPTER 4: ENTERTAINING

Bissell: (416) 453-4451
Black & Decker: (800) 231-9786
Capresso: (800) 767-3554
Cava Stappi Wine Opener: (800) 217-1958
Chantal: (800) 365-4354
Chef's Choice: (800) 342-3255
Holdems: (714) 444-4FUN
MagicKan: (888) 259-7772
Max Burton: (800) 272-8603
Metro: (800) 367-0845
Metrokane: (800) 724-4321
Oinking Snackbowl: (800) 922-3110
OXO: (800) 445-6836
Pool Chip n Dip: (516) 273-2660
Rock n Roll Pizza Cutter: (800) 467-4656
Royal Dirt Devil: (800) 321-1134
Salton: (800) 272-5629
Screwpull: (800) 626-6488
Taco Time: (800) 467-4656
Vesture: (800) 467-4656
Vintage Enhancer: (800) 217-1958

West Bend: (414) 334-2311
Whirley Pop: (800) 270-2705
Wine Butler: (800) WINE TUX
Wolfgang Puck: (800) 275-8273

CHAPTER 5: BIG-TICKET ITEMS

Frigidaire: (800) FRIGIDAIRE
Glowmaster: (800) 272-7008
Jenn-AIRE: (800) JENNAIRE
Kenmore: (800) 359-2000
KitchenAid: (800) 541-6390
Miele: (800) 843-7231
Moen: (800) BUY-MOEN
Sunbeam: (800) 621-8854
Thermador: (800) 656-9226 x 14

CHAPTER 6: HIGH-TECH KITCHEN

Autodesk: (800) 215-9742
Brother: (800) 284-HELP
GE: (800) 211-3089
Kitchen Coach: (800) 897-8554
Mangia: (704) 357-1080
Multicom: (800) 850-7272
Proton: (562) 404-2222
RCA (Home Director): (800) 211-3089
RCA: (800) 336-1900
Sony: (800) 222-SONY
Williams Sonoma: (800) 541-2233